PRAISE FOR

RECEIVING AND GIVING

"My church and I have been living out the BLESS challenge for a number of years now, and it has transformed our lives and our impact on our city. I'm so grateful to Dave Peterson for crystallizing these rhythms in this very accessible resource. It will empower ordinary believers to live lives of extraordinary grace in their neighborhood."

— Michael Frost, author of *The Shaping of Things to Come* and *The Road to Missional*

"Dave Peterson has placed his finger on the gift and the mission that lie at the core of redeemed humanity: 'blessed to be a blessing.' When this mission is forgotten, religion becomes a disaster. When it is remembered, faith again brings hope. When it is lived, it's the power of grace. Dave's own life and ministry are an incarnation of this mission—the most worthwhile mission the human race has yet to receive."

— John Ortberg, Pastor, Menlo Park Presbyterian Church and award-winning author of *The Life You've Always Wanted, When the Game is Over it All Goes Back in the Box,* and other influential books

"Dave Peterson's exploration of 'blessing' is timely and challenging. Certainly, the biblical reality called "blessing" is one of the least understood terms in our Christian vocabulary. Yet there is no facet of our faith that is more important for our faithful witness to God's love at work in human history. Here is a much needed resource that opens up scripture to help us discover the wonders of receiving and giving blessing."

— Darrell Guder, Henry Winters Luce Professor of Missional and Ecumenical Theology Princeton Theological Seminary and leading scholar in Missional theology

"I can think of few people better qualified to challenge us to be a blessing to others than my friend Dave Peterson. Dave has been that all his life. His authenticity, sharp biblical insights, and rich illustrations will help you better embrace God's call of blessing others with your life. I highly recommend this book."

— Dr. Robert Lewis, Founder, Men's Fraternity and bestselling author of *The Quest for Authentic Manhood; Raising a Modern Day Knight.*

"David Peterson has spent his entire adult life distinguishing himself as one of the great preachers, teachers, and leaders of the church, as evidenced by the steady growth of every church he has served as senior pastor. But more than that, he has also pondered what it means for ordinary Christians to follow Jesus, thus making discipleship the call of the many rather than simply the call of the few. More than anyone I know, David has learned how to apply the Christian faith to daily life. His new book, *Receiving and Giving: Unleashing the BLESS Challenge in Your Life*, comes after years of reflection and embodies 'best thoughts and practices' on what it means for ordinary people to live as disciples. It puts abstract theology into livable principles. I am confident it will have a significant impact."

— Gerald L. Sittser, Professor of Theology, Whitworth University, and author of *A Grace Disguised, A Grace Revealed*, and *Water From a Deep Well*

"The power of a good teacher comes from the experience and knowledge of his own authentic journey. Dave Peterson is one of the worthy guides. May these pages be their own blessing."

— Paula D'Arcy, speaker, retreat facilitator, and author of *Red Fire, A Quest for Awakening, Gift of the Red Bird, A Spiritual Encounter*, and many other books

"As I look back over my life, I think of the many blessings God has bestowed on me. They have come in many forms such as good health, a good education, a great family, good fortune, and good friends. But one of the best is my friendship with Dave Peterson. As a servant of God and a student of the scriptures, he has the ability to communicate his insight through his preaching and writing as if you are the only person he is talking to. That is truly a blessing not many possess."

— Robert McNair, owner of The Houston Texans

"The Reverend David Peterson is, of all the preachers I have been privileged to hear, the Master Illustrator. This rich gift now watermarks every page of his brand new book *Receiving and Giving*. David was our family's Pastor at The First Presbyterian Church of Spokane from 1988 through 1995. Now in this book he has become Pastor to the World in his master illustration on How To Be A Blessing."

— Frederick Dale Bruner, George & Lyda Wasson Professor of Religion, Whitworth College (retired), international Bible teacher and author of *Matthew: A Commentary* and *John: A Commentary*

"I am delighted to commend my friend Dave Peterson's *Receiving and Giving*. In compelling ways and words, Dave challenges all of us to live out the meaning of the biblical injunction 'blessed to be a blessing.' Nurtured out of a pastor's heart, written by one of our finest preachers, the book invites us into a fresh conversation about the meaning of stewardship."

— Ronald C. White, Jr., Chaplin, Whitworth University; Dean, San Francisco Theological Seminary and author of *A. Lincoln: A Biography* and *Lincoln's Greatest Speech: The Second Inaugural*

"One of the surest indicators of spiritual health is the balance between being a person who both gives and receives. Dave Peterson hits the nail on the head in this remarkable book!"

— Chris Seay, Ecclesia Church, author of
A Place at the Table

"David and Terri Peterson are some of the most spirit-filled people I have ever encountered. In his book, *Receiving and Giving: Unleashing the BLESS Challenge in Your Life*, David has done a fabulous job laying out the principles he and Terri have lived by in their community and before a vast congregation. It will do you well to read this book."

— Luis Palau, World Evangelist

RECEIVING AND
GIVING

Unleashing the **BLESS Challenge** in Your Life

DAVID A. PETERSON

ACKNOWLEDGMENTS

My life has been redefined by the kindness of God. Saint Paul began his Letter to the Romans by offering a grim description of the human condition. After a full chapter of despair, the letter turns to Chapter Two and the surprising announcement: *Do you not know that it is the kindness of the Lord that is meant to turn your life around?* (Romans 2:4). Kindness is God's grand scheme for changing the world.

God's kindness has been extended to me through the circumstance of my birth to godly parents, Donald and Eleanor Peterson; by allowing my path to join that of my beloved wife, Terri; by bringing children forth from our love—Traci, Anji, Kevin, and Grant, and through them (and their spouses Jon, Josh, Nicola, and Ellen), grandchildren Alex, Megan, Brian, and Nathan.

God has kindly immersed my whole life in the environment of Jesus' blessings found in His Church.

The seed for this book was planted in a comment made by Michael Frost, the influential missional thinker, who described to me how the small groups in his Australian congregation have worked for years to bless the community around them.

That comment got me wondering about blessings—their origin, their shape, their boundaries, and their impact. The word "bless" is common and familiar to us, and yet little attention has been given to its definition. This book is one man's attempt to do just that. In our increasingly secular culture where Christians live more and more on the margins, *Receiving and Giving: Unleashing the BLESS Challenge in Your Life* outlines a lifestyle of distinction that brings transformation through kindness.

I must acknowledge the indelible impact of the congregations I have served and the remarkable people in them whose fingerprints are on every page: First Presbyterian Church, Reardan, Washington; First Presbyterian Church, Elko, Nevada; First Presbyterian Church, Grand Haven, Michigan; First Presbyterian Church, Spokane, Washington; and Memorial Drive Presbyterian Church (MDPC), Houston, Texas.

I cannot imagine a better laboratory for investigating this topic than the community of pastors here at MDPC— Dave Steane, Brett Hurst, Kristin Huffman, Vicky Jones, Brandon Gaide, Rachel Poysky, Rick Myers, and Mauricio

Chacon, all of whose brainstorming and encouragement have added immeasurably to this project. And every day, Becky Weatherall and Gena Kooken have simplified my life so I could devote time to writing. Beyond that, the elders and leadership of this great church have always kept the light green so I could continue moving forward.

Along the way, Dale and Kathy Bruner have taught me never to let go of the Bible, and my Monday Men's Group has demonstrated more of the kindness of the Lord than I could ever have imagined. Through the decades, Jim and Wanda Cowles, Bob and Janice McNair, Jack and Marguerite Baldwin, Steve and Sheila Miller, David and Bonnie Weekley, L.P. and Naomi Jones, Joe and Billie Carole McMillan, David Spaw, and Sam and Norma Gainer have been trailblazers for us.

I would have given up long ago except for the constant encouragement of Terri, the chief blessing in my life. Her influence and edits are on every page. I'm also grateful to Ralph Wheeler, Christyn Soland, Ginny Glass, Doug Gehrman, Eva Kaminski and Linda Illg for reading and making comments and to Becky Weatherall and her small group for taking a year to work through these pages.

Every thought on every page, every breath taken, every keystroke, every insight owes its existence to the *kindness of the Lord*. This *kindness* is behind every blessing and the sum total of these blessings is the great power that God will use to change history.

DEDICATION

To Terri, the most grace-filled agent of God's blessings I have ever known.

To Traci and Anji whose faces, voices and touch profoundly bless me and so many others each day and to Kevin and Grant whose remarkable artistic gifts and creative vision bless the world with beauty and make the cover of this book its best part.

and

To the churches I have served, especially Memorial Drive Presbyterian Church, the personification of The Bless Challenge.

CONTENTS

INTRODUCTION

There are 31,173 verses in the Bible, and I can summarize them all in two verses.

I will bless you…
so that you will be a blessing…
and in you all the families of the earth will be blessed.
(Genesis 12:2-3)

I've always thought of the Bible as a string of time bombs. Certain verses are programmed to explode with meaning at precise moments in our lives. A few years ago, this passage blew up in my mind. God's plan for transforming history is contained in the power of blessings.

Bear with me while I do some counting. The first eleven chapters of the Bible make two things undeniably clear. First, God loves freedom, and second, people can't handle the freedom God loves. God loves freedom because it's the only atmosphere in which love can breathe and God is love (1 John 4:8).

But this freedom proves impossible for people to manage. We're not 62 verses into the Bible's history before men and women are second-guessing God and hiding from Him. We're not 88 verses in before men are killing each other. We're not 143 verses in before:

The LORD saw that the wickedness of humankind was great in the earth, and that every inclination of the thoughts of their hearts was only evil continually (Genesis 6:5).

And we're only 160 verses in before God decides to reset history with a flood. In the 200th verse of the Bible, Noah and his family step off the ark and are greeted with a sparkling new day, a refreshed world, and a new beginning. But Noah and his family were still free. And freedom was still a big problem for people to handle. So it comes as little surprise that a scant 70 verses later it is reported that disobedience has once again become people's main occupation. God looks on the tower they are building to reach up to the heavens, and God says:

'Look, they are one people, and they have all one language; and this is only the beginning of what they will do; nothing that they propose to do will now be impossible for them.'
(Genesis 11:6)

In case you're curious, when God said, *this is only the beginning of what they will do; nothing that they propose to do will now be impossible for them,* it wasn't meant as a compliment.

It was an ominous warning. So here we are just 273 verses into the Bible and we've already had the Fall, the Flood, and the Tower of Babel.

So what will God do now? What will be God's strategy for the remaining 30,900 verses of the Bible and for all the other days that will one day fill the pages of human history? How will God bring love and freedom together to redeem history? The answer to that question is the subject of this book, *Receiving and Giving: Unleashing the BLESS Challenge in Your Life.*

In what has to be the most unexpected turn in history, God appeared to a man named Abraham and said:

I will bless you...
so that you will be a blessing...
and in you all the families of the earth will be blessed.
(Genesis 12:2-3)

In the Bible are 475 references to "blessing." Interestingly, there are only 309 references to "pray" and 109 more to "prayer." I take this difference to add gravity to God's commitment to the act of blessing as His central occupation.

Nassim Nicholas Taleb has popularized the Black Swan Theory, which holds that much of life is driven by high impact, hard-to-predict events that are beyond the realm of expectation. Since most swans are white, seeing a black swan always surprises. It is unexpected. It is out-of-the-ordinary.

God's plan to reset history through the transformational power of blessings is history's original black swan. It couldn't have been predicted. No one could see it coming.

This unexpectedness is the mark of a blessing. You don't see it coming. It's out of proportion to its circumstance. It catches you by surprise. It is an occasion where you don't get what you do deserve and do get what you don't deserve.

David Blaine is well-known for his street magic. He has a card trick where he opens a deck of cards and asks a passerby to pick one from the deck. After the choice is made, he throws the deck at a plate glass window of a shop facing out onto the street. The fifty-two cards scatter everywhere, but one actually sticks to the window. And of course, it's the card that was chosen. That in itself is amazing. But when asked to peel the card off the window, the person discovers that the card isn't on the outside of the window, but on the inside! People are stunned. How did he manage to throw fifty-two cards at the outside of a window and get the one chosen card to stick to the inside of that glass? People explode with laughter. They jump up and down. They shake their heads and walk in circles. This means of surprise is how God blesses. Somehow, God manages to do the unexpected. He makes the card stick on the inside of the window, and that's what takes your breath away. That's how blessings work.

God not only intends to bless you this way, but He also wants you to animate His blessing in the world where you live. He intends for you to be His agent of surprise in the affairs and events of people's lives. When I was very young, I carried a small stuffed rabbit in the pocket of my shirt. I would transfer it to the inkwell of my desk at school. It all seems silly now when I think back on it. But in that surreal chapter of my childhood, I dreamed that stuffed rabbit might somehow come to life. God dreams about you coming to life. You are here on planet Earth to bring God's blessings to life—to animate them. What would it be like if God's thoughts and purposes were to soak into your blood until they found expression in the words of your mouth and the touch of your hands? That's *The BLESS Challenge*.

But what do blessings look like? What are their dimensions? We have a vague sense of blessings. People often say, "I'm so blessed," or, "God bless you." But what do these expressions mean? In everyday life, what does it mean to be blessed and to bless others?

I've turned the word "bless" into an acronym that embraces the two great dimensions of blessed living—the dimension of *receiving* (*I will bless you*) and the human dimension of *giving* (*to be a blessing*).

*B*less Everyone

*L*isten to God

*E*at with Someone

*S*tudy Jesus

*S*erve Generously

Those who accept The BLESS Challenge are never bored and never adrift. No matter where they are, no matter who's in front of them, and no matter what challenge they face, they always find an opportunity to receive and give God's blessings in practical and compelling ways.

The world you live in right now needs someone like you to bless it. You are designed by God to receive and to pass along His blessings. The BLESS Challenge is designed to sharpen the way you think and live in the world. God's desire is to make the world a better place through you. The transformation of the world begins with your own transformation. The more broadly you receive and apply these principles across the whole range of your life, the more naturally you will transmit them into your corner of the world.

I've travelled the globe and seen its poverty, disease, violence, and unrest. The size and scale of it depresses me. It makes me want to hide. After all, what can one person do? But I've also seen hope at work, and hope is always driven by one person. The power is not in the size or number; it's in the vision. The greatest power in the world is the power of one. That's what makes blessings so surprisingly potent.

The BLESS Challenge defines and energizes the power of the individual. Not long ago, NASA launched its feeblest spacecraft ever, called *Dawn*. Its target was deep space. The great challenge the scientists faced was providing enough fuel. Conventional rocketry would require an impossible amount of fuel to travel such a great distance. So the scientists devised a new kind of engine and an alternative fuel. Once the spacecraft escaped earth's gravity, it switched to a booster that accelerated at the nearly immeasurably slow rate of 15 mph per day. That's why NASA described it as its feeblest spacecraft. But if you do the math, you discover that by continuing to accelerate at 15 mph/day, you will eventually reach *Dawn's* cruising speed of 24,500 mph, making it one of NASA's fastest spacecrafts. Small deeds sustained over long days have astonishing potential.

When God hit the reset button on history, He did so by commissioning one man—Abraham. *In you all the families of the earth shall be blessed* (Genesis 12:3). That one, single, solitary man began his slow acceleration into history. And now, 4,000 years later, like the spacecraft *Dawn*, the impact of that one man's life has transformed peoples and nations and redirected the very trajectory of history itself. The impact of Abraham's life is still being felt today.

The longest enduring legacy you can leave with your life is the way you bless others. It's true that we're all broken people. And it's obvious that our brokenness leaves a trail of trouble for others. But by God's design, the impact of our brokenness disappears after a few generations and is replaced by the impact of the blessings we leave behind. The Bible says:

> *...the blessings of God extend to a thousand generations of*
> *those who love Him and keep His commandments.*
>
> (Deuteronomy 7:9)

I tried to calculate the math for how long those blessings would endure. If God has designed a blessing to last a thousand generations and a generation is measured as thirty years, that means that by blessing others, your life can have an impact for good that's still being felt 30,000 years from now. Imagine that!

So let's get started. As you read along, you'll notice a scattering of "dialogue boxes." I've borrowed this term from interactive technology. The boxes give you direction on how to apply the BLESS Challenge in your life. They offer suggestions for reflection, meditation, memorization, and action. I hope they help bring blessings to life in your life.

DIALOGUE BOX

Your journal

List what you understand to be the five greatest blessings in your life.

Your prayers

Give thanks to God for these blessings.

Your discussion

- Compared to others, what do you find distinctive about your blessings? What do you think this distinction means?

- Describe some of the qualities that you think distinguish a good deed from a true blessing.

Your memory

Genesis 12:1-3

Your action

- Make a list of the reasons you think you are undeserving of God's blessings. Now repeat to yourself, *God blesses me anyway.*

- Write a note to the person (alive or dead) who has blessed your life the most.

PART ONE

BLESS EVERYONE

Blessings redefine reality. God blesses us by stretching an astonishing new reality to cover us. Reality argues that we are invisible, a blip, a vapor. Even the slightest change in social atmosphere can make us disappear. So when the Psalmist says:

> *When I consider the heavens, the works of your fingers,*
> *the moon and the stars that You have made*
> **I wonder...who am I that you should notice me?**
> (Psalm 8:3-4)

Indeed! Absolutely! Without question! I wonder:

> *Who am I that You should notice me?*

Blessed by being noticed by God

Why should God notice us? After all, we are so small. We are specks of dust in the vast cosmic cloud. If you've ever sat where the morning sun streams into a room and noticed a speck of reflected dust floating in the light, that's you or me. Blink and we're gone. We occupy a planet that revolves around a mid-sized star. This star is only one of 400 billion stars in our Milky Way galaxy and our Milky Way galaxy is only one of an estimated 500 billion galaxies that make up the universe. With a super-sized calculator you may be able to wrap the mathematics around the scale of the universe, but you can't wrap your mind around it.

And on this obscure planet Earth, I am a single needle in a vast human haystack made up of 7 billion other needles. Each of these "needles" has hopes and dreams. Each struggles and strives to survive. Experts calculate that the average person thinks somewhere between 12,000 and 30,000 thoughts a day. If there are 7 billion people on planet Earth and each person thinks 30,000 thoughts a day, how can God possibly keep track of me and the thoughts I think and the hopes I carry and the temptations I face? The Psalmist asks the most obvious question:

> *I wonder…what are human beings that you are mindful of*
> *them,*
> *mortals that you care for them?*
> (Psalm 8:4)

I wonder whether God can keep track of me? I wonder whether God really knows my name. I wonder whether He really cares about what I care about. I wonder whether He is actually involved in the details of my life. I wonder whether managing the vast scale of galaxies and planets doesn't somehow completely exhaust or thoroughly preoccupy the Creator, leaving no time for me.

As the Breton fisherman's prayer puts it, *"O God, Thy sea is so great and my boat is so small."* The one thing that would not surprise me in such a vast and complex universe is to be unnoticed.

And more than being small, at my best I am unremarkable, and at my worst, I am the kind of person you would think God would want to forget. Perhaps some people capture God's attention, really remarkable people like the Pope or Billy Graham, but not me. Once, I was visiting with a friend. We had been working on a project. I had written a document containing my best thinking. When the document came up in the conversation, my friend rolled his desk chair across the floor and reached into this trash can to retrieve my crumpled paper. Like a hot iron, he tried to flatten out the wrinkled paper with his fist. He smiled, pointed at the trash can, and said, "That's my Dave Peterson file." The painful and sobering truth is that even at my best I am so— unremarkable. So utterly forgettable.

The assembly line of my mind churns out thousands of reasons why it cannot be possible that God notices me in light of the obscurity of my being and the thoughts I think and the things I do. Why would God notice a man who is so ordinary, obscure, intentionally and habitually disobedient, and so hopelessly self-centered?

That's what makes this news that I am noticed by the Creator God so astonishing. That's what makes it a blessing—it is so unfathomable—so surprising and unexpected. Even the brightest mind working for decades cannot fathom it. It comes from out-of-the-blue. It is out-of-proportion to reality. It bubbles up from the far side. By noticing me, God stretches a vast and wonderful new reality over my existence.

I am visible!

I am not a vapor.

I am somebody.

I AM!

And it's not just that God notices us—He does so in a particular way. He makes note of us in order to bless us.

CHAPTER ONE

THE BLESSING:
God Blesses You by Noticing You and Connecting with You

God doesn't simply notice us—God notices us in particular ways that animate the blessing. The shocking nature of God's attention is that it is so unrelentingly sustained. God never stops noticing us.

> *My help comes from the Lord,*
> *who made heaven and earth.*
>
> *He will not let your foot be moved;*
> *he who keeps you will not slumber.*
> *He who keeps Israel*
> *will neither slumber nor sleep.*
>
> *The Lord is your keeper;*
> *the Lord is your shade at your right hand.*
> *The sun shall not strike you by day,*
> *nor the moon by night.*
>
> *The Lord will keep you from all evil;*
> *he will keep your life.*
> *The Lord will keep*

> *your going out and your coming in*
> *from this time on and for evermore.*
> (Psalm 121:3-8)

God's blessings never slumber nor sleep

In light of the obscurity of my size and the unremarkable nature of my life, I cannot fathom how God's radar works. North America has NORAD to track all atmospheric activities. Satellites, radar installations, and sound monitors keep track of even the slightest movements. Apparently, God has His own surveillance system to keep track of me. The Bible makes no effort to describe God's tracking system. The Bible makes no attempt to explain how God can possibly know my thoughts before I think them, and my words before I speak them, and my days before I live them (Psalm 139). The Bible doesn't debate this process; it simply declares that it is true. It does not come as a proposition; it comes as a pronouncement.

God is my keeper!

God never slumbers!

God never sleeps!

Blessed by God as a nursing child

> *Can a woman forget her nursing-child,*
> *or show no compassion for the child of her womb?*
> *Even these may forget,*

yet I will not forget you.
(Isaiah 49:15)

God notices us as a mother would her nursing child. How can it be described more intimately than that? My wife, Terri, has tried to describe what the experience of nursing is like, but she's not far along into the explanation before she runs out of words. God does not know us by our social security number or our member ID. He knows us as a mother knows a nursing child.

There are lots of ways to notice people: critically, analytically, leeringly, passingly, objectively, fretfully, guardedly, obsessively, indifferently—but the way God notices us is as a mother notices a nursing child. It is so physical. It is so intimate. It is so proximate. It's so mutual. It's so satisfying. It's so life-giving. It's so tender. It's so—Divine!

God's blessings never forget you

When an infant is abandoned, the story makes the news because people wonder, "How could a mother do that?" But God says that it's more likely for a mother to abandon a nursing child than that He should ever abandon you.

Even these may forget,
yet I will not forget you.
(Isaiah 49:15)

God gives us these analogies to stretch our concept of reality, not that even these analogies really ensure that we'll get it. The truth is that we can't think our way to understanding the depth and width and height and breadth of God's intimate connection to us. Stephen Hawking is one of the smartest people around. He's stretched his mind to its limit on this subject and has concluded, rationally speaking, that there can be no God. Like the Psalmist, Hawking has spent most of his life wondering about the design of the universe and the place of humans in it. In his book, *The Grand Design,* Hawking wrote that, "God did not create the universe…the universe can and will create itself from nothing." In a recent interview, Hawking went on to say "There is no heaven or afterlife…that is a fairy story for people afraid of the dark." Here is a great mind that cannot fathom either the existence or the care of God. Hawking has concluded that we come from nothing and we return to nothing. For him, NOTHING is the centering reality of life.

But just because a brilliant mind can't conceive of God does not mean that God doesn't exist; it simply means that God's reality exceeds the intellect and imagination of the human mind.

So in a form that exceeds intellect, God notices you and connects with you in a way more permanently unbreakable than the bond between a nursing mother with child. God has loved you every second of every minute of every day of your life. Here is where God's blessing begins in my life—and in yours!

Inscribed blessings

God notices you with intensity.

See, I have inscribed you on the palms of My hands;
(Isaiah 49:15-16)

Where the Riverside State Park curls along the shoreline of the Spokane River in Northeastern Washington is a wooden picnic shelter. It's near the place in the river they call The Bowl and Pitcher. When you look at the ceiling, you see names, hundreds of them, perhaps thousands. Who knows when the tradition started, but now they are layered on top of each other, etched in the wood, written in crayon, chalk, and ink. When I stand there looking up, I feel like I'm looking at the palm of God's hands.

God chooses His words carefully. If He doesn't, He's easily misunderstood. So God says, *I have etched* (inscribed) *you on the palm of my hands.* I am not just a name written on a list of paper. A list can get lost. You can leave a list in a pocket of your blue jeans and have it dissolve in the laundry. And I am not even a tattoo on God's palm. It's true that a tattoo will last a lifetime, but even so, it's not permanent. Even a tattoo can be removed. No, God carefully chooses the word *etched/inscribed* to describe His connection to me. It is a graphic term. You are like a scar on God's hand. You are permanent!

To understand the implications of this statement, I did a bit of research on the practice of scarification. It's an ancient tradition that has developed a certain global popularity in our present-day. It involves cutting the skin to produce a permanent scar. In certain tribes in the Sudan, the head is shaved and six rings are cut around the head. But that's only the tip of the scarification iceberg. Google offers an abundance of websites that show the dramatic effects of this practice that is known as "etching" or "inscribing"—the same words God uses:

> *See, I have inscribed you on the palms of my hands;*
> (Isaiah 49:15-16)

I squirmed to watch the procedure. First came the cutting of the design to create a wound, and second was the repeated irritation of the wound further to dramatize the scar. In other words, the more the scab is picked, the more dramatic the inscription becomes. Is this process what God means? Am I like a scar to Him? Am I an irritated wound to God that does not break the relationship but only deepens it, making it even more beautiful in time?

God's connection to us is not only warm and tender like a mother nursing a child; it is also fierce and deep, like a wound that with time and repeated irritation produces a beautiful scar. When Jesus appeared to the disciples after His crucifixion, the first thing He showed Thomas were the scars on His hands and feet and side. And somehow, unless you glimpse the graphic nature of God's devotion toward you, you don't really get it. If the description of the attention God pays to you doesn't somehow make you squirm, if it doesn't cut the skin and make you bleed, if it doesn't make you shake your head and want to turn away, you haven't grasped it.

*See, I have **inscribed** you on the palms of my hands;*
(Isaiah 49:15-16)

You are not some name on a list that can be lost or laundered. You are not a tattoo that is here-today-and-gone-tomorrow. You are a scar on God. You are inscribed on Him—permanently. And even the pain and irritation that you may cause Him only intensifies the beauty of the part you play in His life.

A few years ago, I sat watching the Player's Golf Championship. Adam Scott took a comfortable two-stroke lead into the last hole of the tournament. After a good drive off the tee, the picture on the television screen shifted to somewhere in the club house where a skilled engraver was etching Adam Scott's name onto a crystal trophy. A-D-A-M... Everyone assumed Scott would win. But then, inexplicably, he pulled his second shot into the water hazard. As the ball disappeared and the ripples widened, the picture shifted back to the engraver. Had he started to engrave too soon? But his steady hand kept engraving—S-C-O....After taking a penalty, Scott hit a poor third shot that was left ten feet from the cup. Two bad shots and Scott's lead was evaporating. The picture shifted back to the club house. The engraver never looked up and his steady hand finished the script T-T just as Adam Scott sank a difficult 10-foot bogey putt for the win.

Whether you are on your game or off, in the fairway or in the hazard, putting for a birdie or putting for a bogey, in the act of winning or the process of losing, faithfully obedient or habitually disobedient… God says:

> *See, I have inscribed you on the palms of my hands;*
> (Isaiah 49:15-16)

These are the amazing dimensions of God's blessing. To God, you are unforgettable; you are a nursing child whose name is inscribed on His hand. These announcements are designed by God to redefine your reality with His blessing.

CHAPTER TWO

THE APPLICATION:
Bless Others by Noticing and Connecting with Them

Since we have been blessed by God for the purpose of blessing others, His act of blessing us by noticing us requires a response.

By definition, blessings exist outside the world of the expected. That's the secret of their power to redefine reality for others. Blessings begin when you notice others in the way God has noticed you. It's not necessarily natural to notice people. In fact, we refine the art of not noticing others. You know the routine of touching without feeling, looking without seeing, and hearing without listening. Blinders protect and preserve our isolation and indifference. People dissolve into objects to be used and not blessed.

Blessing others begins by noticing them and assuming that no one in your life is there by accident. No one! Life has a thousand ways to hide people in its dark folds. For example, Anne Mahlum's morning run through the streets of Philadelphia took her past a homeless shelter. As the men got used to seeing her each morning, they offered smiles and greetings. One day in July 2007, Anne wondered to herself why she just ran by these men every day. It was as if she actually saw them for the first time. And with that, she rounded up some shoes and shorts and invited the men to run with her. And that's how the *Back on My Feet* running club got started. "Running is such a beautiful metaphor for life. Life is about choosing different roads filled with opportunity, hope, and happiness," says Anne. The goal is a revived and re-energized view of life. Anne Mahlum is busy noticing forgotten people, bringing them back to life, and stretching over them a new reality.

Connect with people who seem lost in the nooks and crannies of life. You'll find them lost in crowds, in poverty, in sickness, in crime, in despair. The sea of life is so large, and so many are drifting in tiny forgotten boats. Remember them. It's an act of blessing.

Our daughter Traci did a social work internship in the Holocaust Museum in Houston. An old soldier described to her the day his unit liberated a concentration camp. They were paralyzed by the impossible extent of hunger, thirst, filth, disease, and despair that met them inside the barbed wire. They didn't even know where to start. Their paltry supplies were irrelevant in the face of the enormity of the need. The old soldier recounted how, nearly sixty years before, he had approached a prisoner who looked like a dead man walking and simply hugged him. It's all he could think to do. And that's when he said the most extraordinary thing happened—a line formed—not for food or water or medical aid, but for a hug. There's power in one person connecting with others.

I turned down the hallway of a hotel one day. A man was walking toward me. When he got closer, I stepped to the side to let him pass at just the moment he did the same. So I stepped to the other side of the hallway, and he did the same. It was an awkward moment. I couldn't get past him. And that's when I actually looked at the man and really noticed him. He was dressed like me, he was tall like me, his hair was like mine, his face was like mine. I realized the man I was looking at—was me. I was walking toward a mirror. I had gotten in the way of myself. Self-preoccupation becomes a roadblock to moving blessings into the world.

The BLESS Challenge begins when we fill our lives with windows instead of mirrors. It begins when we notice people and connect with them.

Bless strangers by noticing them

Blessings stretch into the world of strangers breaking down barriers, which requires an important mental adjustment in the way we look at other people. Our human nature easily views others either as tools for getting what we want or as obstacles standing in the way of getting what we want. The BLESS Challenge requires a sustained recalibration of attitude toward strangers. We can no longer look at strangers as tools or obstacles. Instead, they must become to us as exotic new territory to be explored and enjoyed. As the Bible says:

Do not neglect to show hospitality to strangers, for by doing that some have entertained angels without knowing it.
(Hebrews 13:2)

I don't know if this verse means that blessing strangers changes them or changes us by changing the way we see them—either way I guess I don't much care. I just know that blessing strangers has transformational power to change us both.

An act becomes a blessing when it invades unfamiliar territory. We live in a vast sea of strangers. In this vast sea, we occupy small, private islands of friendship. Blessings occur when we invade the islands of strangers with the unlimited and unexpected favor of God. When we do, we discover that life moves at the speed of friendship.

Randy Joubert knew he'd been adopted as an infant. Curiosity about his past drove him to search the State of Maine's database for information about his past. He discovered he had a brother, but because the names had been changed, he had no idea how to find him. Six months later, Randy, who worked as a furniture deliveryman, was assigned a new coworker. It seemed to everyone that Gary Nisbet looked a lot like Randy and they had so many similar quirks and traits that it felt eerie. Customers kept asking, "Are you two brothers?" And it turns out they were. For thirty-five years, they had lived in the same town without knowing of the other. Gradually, Randy realized that the man who had been on the other end of countless couches, mattresses, and recliners for the previous six months wasn't just a co-worker. He was the long-lost brother for whom Randy had been searching. Randy certainly hadn't expected to discover that the man working next to him was his brother. This new discovery has transformed not only the way Randy and Gary work with each other; the whole company reports an atmospheric transformation. That's what happens when we see strangers in a different way.

It also happened when Denver Moore asked Ron Hall a question. Ron was rich and volunteered at the homeless shelter where Denver was a resident. When Ron tried to befriend him, Denver asked whether he was interested in a real friendship or a "catch and release" relationship. Somehow "poor" Denver could see that "rich" Ron saw him as some combination of tool and obstacle. It took years of work and gallons of coffee, but the breakthrough finally came when Denver and Ron saw each other as real human beings. And then blessings began to flow between these two strangers.

Everyone knows what it's like to be treated as a tool or an obstacle. Unfortunately, it's the treatment we expect from strangers. So when they treat us like we are real, it's surprising and it feels like—a blessing.

Bless enemies by noticing them

Remember the old counsel, "Stay close to your friends and closer to your enemies." It applies to blessings as well. Blessings bless because they can be so elastic and can stretch into places we'd never think possible. An act takes on the characteristics of a blessing when it goes a step further than anyone expects. Nowhere is this truth more evident than in the way blessings stretch toward enemies. This point is what Paul was getting at when he wrote:

> *Bless those who persecute you; bless and do not curse them…*
> *If your enemies are hungry, feed them; if they are thirsty,*
> *give them something to drink; for by doing this you will heap*
> *burning coals on their heads. Do not be overcome by evil,*
> *but overcome evil with good.*
> (Romans 12:14, 20-21)

The part about *heaping burning coals upon their heads* sounds more like a curse than a blessing. But it was really an old figure of speech meaning: inflame their conscience. That's what persistent acts of blessing do. Everyone knows what it's like when someone is unusually kind toward you—and especially an enemy. It surprises you. You can't get it off your mind. It creates a whole new environment. The blessing of enemies has been one of the most powerful transformative forces in history. When you go the extra mile, when you offer the unexpected gift, that's when the blessing moves out of the nursery and into graduate school.

In the fourteenth century, Koud Naba, the local chief of the village of Bazoule, a community outside modern day Burkina Faso's capital Ouagodougou, determined that the village's ancient enemy, the Nile Crocodile, was sacred. Nile Crocodiles are the largest in the world, but by giving the crocs their fill of chickens, the villagers gradually calmed the ancient animosity. Today, crocodiles and children live side-by-side. Tourists flock to the village to see and touch these ancient enemies. Rather than fearing the crocodiles, they bless them. It makes headlines when enemies become friends.

Blessings are designed to reach into hostile territory to bring healing. The happiest endings and greatest blessings in life are reserved for enemies who in the end become friends.

DIALOGUE BOX

Your journal

Write about the main roadblocks in your life to noticing and connecting with others.

Your prayers

Pray Ephesians 3:18-19, repeating it over and over for five minutes.

Your discussion

- How do you respond to the idea that God notices you in intimate and detailed ways as described in this chapter?

- Discuss the main reasons why noticing and connecting with others makes you apprehensive.

Your memory

Isaiah 49:15-16

Your action

- Make a list of "invisible" people in your life.

- In what ways might you bless them by noticing them?

CHAPTER THREE

THE BLESSING:
God Blesses You by Going One Step Further

God notices us in a way that redefines our reality, especially the broken and painful parts of it, the parts of our lives that are hardest for us to bear. God is willing to go as far as He must and do as much as it takes to bless us.

By nature, blessings are elastic. They stretch new reality into new territory. God's blessings show up where people don't expect them on occasions that are surprising. Blessings substantially change reality by stretching into new territory and surrounding unlikely people with acts of goodness that they don't expect.

God's blessings penetrate to the heart of life

In one of the *Superman* movies, there's a scene where Superman is having a conversation with Lois Lane. She's confused about where he's been and what he's been doing. He takes hold of her and they rise high above the city, above its noise and clamor. Superman asks Lois, "Do you hear that?" She answers, "I don't hear anything. What do you hear?" Superman answers, "I hear everything." Superman's line carries a biblical dimension. When God says, "your walls are before Me" (Isaiah 49:15-16), He means for us to know that He hears, sees, and understands everything. The walls that God mentions are the walls that stretched around Jerusalem. These walls were thick and high. Israel was very proud of the beautiful strong walls it had built around itself. The walls announced, "Israel is great. Israel is strong. Israel has God's favor. Israel cannot be broken." But Israel became proud. Israel lost its way. Israel pulled away from God. And God let the people go because love does not insist on its own way. Along came the Babylonians. And the Babylonians pulled down Israel's walls and left them lying there in great ruins. They also rounded up most of the able-bodied population and took them off to Babylon as slaves. They left behind the people who had neither the strength nor the resources to rebuild the walls. And there the walls lay for two generations. The ruined walls constantly reminded Israel of its rebellion and the loss of the glory that might have been.

Our son, Grant, begged for a BB gun. He was young and we said, "No, you'll shoot your eye out—or something else." But he continued to beg and promise to be careful so we relented. We gave the gun with a warning, "You can only shoot the gun when we go out in the country." The next day, my office phone rang. It was Grant's older brother, Kevin, calling to say that Grant had shot out the glass slider on the deck—the most expensive window in the house. Our kitchen table was just inside the window, so because only the outer pane had broken and the glass company couldn't come for a couple of days, we ate all of our meals in the shadow of the broken glass. The BB had broken the outer pane into a spider web of tiny fragments that continued to splinter and fall like tiny hailstones rattling against the frame. It was a constant reminder of disobedience. Such were the broken-down walls of Jerusalem. For two generations, they lay there, announcing to the world the shame of Jerusalem.

God blesses our tears

So here's the picture. Our broken-down walls are ever before God. God is always aware of our brokenness, always aware of our vulnerability, always aware of our shame, always aware of our loss, our broken promises, our disobedience or intentional rebellion.

Try to understand the implications of this situation for God—our brokenness is always before God. God does not turn away from our brokenness. If it were me, I'd rather not look. I'd rather not see. I'd rather keep walking with my big protective blinders in place. I wish I'd never seen the beggar on the street corner. I'd rather not know the trouble others are in. I'd rather not know their suffering. Once you see something or know about it, you can't unsee it; you cannot unknow it. Because when you see or know, then you are faced with the dilemma of acting or ignoring. But this is God, and God blesses by noticing our brokenness. As the Psalmist says:

> *You have kept count of my tossings;*
> *put my tears in your bottle.*
> *Are they not in your record?*
> (Psalm 56:8)

A young man had graduated from seminary. He had big plans to travel to Europe and start a retreat center where people could gather for spiritual renewal. Bags in hand, he walked toward the train station on the first leg of his dream. But his way was blocked by a beggar lying in the street. To get to his dream, the young man had to step over the beggar. But he couldn't do it because once you see something, you can't unsee it. And so instead, he walked down the street, bought a small gas stove, and boiled a bag of rice to feed the man—and a line formed. That was the beginning of what today has become the largest Christian service agency for homeless people in Seoul, South Korea. In that moment of decision, Pastor Choi did a perfect impression of God.

God never steps over us in our trouble. God never turns a blind eye to our need. God is never insensitive to our broken dreams. God is not put off by the consequences of our rebellion. Our walls are ever before Him.

Humpty Dumpty sat on a wall,
Humpty Dumpty had a great fall.
All the king's horses and all the king's men
Couldn't put Humpty together again.

As bad as things were for Humpty Dumpty, they are even worse for us because it's not only we who have fallen off the wall—the wall itself has fallen. Who will put us back together again?

Blue collar blessings

God will put us back together. It is the nature of His work of blessing. For God, blessing us is blue collar work. He rolls up His sleeves and digs into the reconstruction project.

Then the LORD said, 'I have observed the misery of my people who are in Egypt; I have heard their cry on account of their taskmasters. Indeed, I know their sufferings, and I have come down to deliver them from the Egyptians, and to bring them up out of that land to a good and broad land, a land flowing with milk and honey.
(Exodus 3:7-8)

God *observes*! God *hears*! God *knows*! And then God *comes to deliver*.

At the end of the block in the small town where I grew up stood a two-stall garage for the volunteer fire department. On the roof, a cluster of speakers aimed north, south, east, and west. At 7 a.m. and 7 p.m., the siren blew once. You could set your clock by it. But if there were ever a fire, the siren would blow seven times. And then you could hear in the distance of north, south, east, and west, the sound of engines starting and tires squealing and gravel spinning as the volunteer firefighters scrambled to the fire. At the siren's sound, they dropped everything and scrambled to help. Whenever trouble comes and our walls are broken, the siren sounds and God comes to deliver.

And at the very moment when you think you've gone so far that God won't bless you, He does.

This blessing of God redefines our reality. God notices us as a nursing mother notices a child, as a bridegroom notices the bride. We are inscribed on God; our troubles are known to Him, and with lights and sirens, He comes to deliver us. What a God! What a blessing!

CHAPTER FOUR
THE APPLICATION:
Bless Others by Going
One Step Further

There's a Hebrew worship song entitled "Dayenu." It means: *It would have been enough for us.* The first five stanzas focus on specific ways God delivers, and after each stanza comes the proclamation, *It would have been enough.* The second five stanzas focus on God's miracles and after each one comes the announcement: *It would have been enough.* Then come five stanzas on the ways God comes to meets us personally, and after each the declaration: *It would have been enough.* God always does MORE than enough. God always exceeds our expectations. Blessings are excessive! Blessings are more than enough. Blessings go a step farther than people expect.

Bless in generous excess

The Bless Challenge stretches a new reality over your life, causing you to live toward others with expanding generosity. After all, generosity is the secret of life. Living with excessive generosity taps you into the secret world of God's limitless supply. The more you give, the more God supplies you to give. It's a phenomenon that can only be known through experience.

When Isaac was looking for a wife, he sent his most trusted servant to search for her. He prayed that God would help him recognize her by her generosity. His prayer was very specific:

> *Let the girl to whom I shall say, "Please offer your jar that I may drink," and who shall say, "Drink, and I will water your camels"—let her be the one whom you have appointed for your servant Isaac. By this I shall know that you have shown steadfast love to my master.*
> (Genesis 24:13-14)

And before the man even finished praying, Rebekah appeared. She asked not only if she could draw water for him, but she went a big step further and offered to draw water for his camels—all twelve of them. I am told that a camel drinks between thirty and fifty gallons at a time. And Rebekah offered to water all twelve of the camels. That's an act of courtesy on steroids. That's going the extra mile. Her extra effort changed her life. It changed Isaac's life. It even changed history itself. Be the person who waters others' camels.

In 1979, Larry Stewart was down on his luck. For the second time in two years, he had been fired from his job a few days before Christmas. When a woman he knew only as "Cookie" gave him a free Christmas dinner, it changed his life. Her simple act of generosity impacted him profoundly. Over the next few years, he made a small fortune in telecommunications. He never forgot Cookie's generosity, so at Christmas, he began disguising himself as Santa Claus and handing out money to needy strangers. He targeted the very people whose luck had run out, who had stepped outside the circle of blessings. He became known as the "Secret Santa," and over the next twenty-five years, he gave away $1.3 million. He did his best to remain anonymous, but excessive generosity catches people's attention and changes the world.

I'm talking about generosity in excess. Excessive generosity blesses people in ways that transform reality. Routine generosity oils the wheels of ordinary life. Excessive generosity transforms life.

Jesus described it in this way:

> *Do not resist an evildoer. But if anyone strikes you on the right cheek, turn the other also; and if anyone wants to sue you and take your coat, give your cloak as well, and if anyone forces you to go one mile, go also the second mile. Give to everyone who begs from you, and do not refuse anyone who wants to borrow from you.*
> (Matthew 5:39-40)

Live your life like the man proposing to his girlfriend. He made arrangements to fly across country and to have her meet him at the airport. On the airplane, he handed out thirty-six photographs of his girlfriend and thirty-six long-stemmed roses and asked thirty-six total strangers when they got off the plane to find the girl in the photo and give her a long-stemmed rose and walk away. I wonder how long it took before she knew something special was coming. The first rose was expected. The second was a thoughtful bonus. The third was a surprise. But the blessings got started somewhere around rose number four—the rose beyond the expected.

Be the person who keeps handing out roses, and keep doing it beyond the expected until people begin to know what it's like to be blessed.

Bless with excessive forgiveness

Forgiveness causes blessings to glow in the dark. They say you can only live in the present and that you can't change the past or the future, but that's not true. Forgiveness changes both. Forgiveness frees us from what was and introduces us to what can be. Jesus taught that our most urgent responsibility toward others is to forgive. Practical experience also teaches that forgiving is some of the most difficult work that we ever do. That's what makes forgiveness a blessing. It's beyond the expected.

Nicholas Lanza's mother, Michelle, worked on the ninety-seventh floor of building two of the World Trade Center on 9/11. He was seven years old and watched on CNN as the tower came down. Nicolas' life exploded like a marshmallow in a microwave. Gradually, he was consumed by demons of depression, wrath, and unforgiveness. The sun would rise in the morning, but all he could see was black. He retreated further and further into his silent self. The summer before high school, Nicholas went to church camp. He didn't go alone. His mother went with him—or the memory of her. He took that memory everywhere. She was bound to him like a great weight he could never put down. But one evening, some pastors gathered around him and prayed that he would be able to let his mother go. And he was suddenly engulfed in a blinding white light. A voice spoke out of the light, "You belong to Me, My child. You shall no longer be burdened with these chains that you wear about you. You are free." The tremendous burden began to lift and more words formed in his mind: "I love you. Now go and tell others the same."

Nicholas' life had been transformed. The old demons were replaced by a strange and powerful new dream of finding Osama Bin Laden and telling him that he forgave him for the hideous crime he had committed against him. In fact, when he heard that Bin Laden had been killed, Nicholas was crushed because he realized that dream would never come true. By then, Nicholas had come to know and believe that: "Forgiveness was essential to really moving on from my tragic happening. I came to learn this through studying the Word of God, prayer and life-experience."[1]

It's said that you can't change time, but that's not true. Forgiveness has the unique power to change the past, the present, and the future. It releases not only the one forgiven, but also the one who forgives.

It's not easy. There are so many obstacles to forgiving: the size of the wound, the unfairness of the offense, the satisfaction of self-righteous indignation. In the summer of 2009, the back pages of newspapers carried the report of an asteroid striking Jupiter. Astronomers noticed a continent-sized hole in Jupiter's outer atmosphere. Jupiter is the largest planet in our solar system. If you were to combine all the other planets into one, Jupiter would be two-and-a-half times larger. Every earthling should be very grateful that Jupiter is in our solar system. It has such an enormous gravitational field that it attracts all sorts of meteors, meteorites, and asteroids that might otherwise strike planet Earth with catastrophic consequences. Jupiter functions like our solar system's vacuum cleaner, absorbing into itself all sorts of destructive elements. That's what forgiveness does. Forgiveness absorbs into itself things that kill and destroy. That's how forgiveness blesses—like an enormous vacuum cleaner for the offenses of the world. When John the Baptist saw Jesus coming toward him, he cried out, "Behold, the

---

1 *Newsweek*, September 4, 2011.

Lamb of God who takes away the sins of the world" (John 1:19). There is no greater or more powerful blessing than to forgive others.

Bless your family, your neighborhood, your office, your church, and your friends by being Jupiter to them, slow to condemn and quick to forgive, absorbing into your atmosphere the brokenness of life.

A fire broke out near our home at a small manufacturing business. Except for a small metal shed, the business burned to the ground. Early the next morning, I drove by the fire site. A fire engine was still there, and smoke was curling up from the tangle of collapsed steel. But out near the street, almost in the lanes of traffic, was an A-frame sign of blackened metal with spray-painted letters scrawled across announcing, "WE'RE STILL OPEN!" Life's complications present us with all sorts of reasons not to keep the flow of blessings flowing from God through us and into the world. Bless others even when people don't expect you to, even when life's difficulties give you every reason not to. No matter what circumstance you find yourself in, bless excessively.

DIALOGUE BOX

Your journal

Write down how you would feel about a person who blessed you in ways that exceeded expectations.

Your prayers

Describe to God the things you are grateful for—things great and small.

Your discussion

- Discuss some of the things that amplify a blessing and increase its impact.

- In what area of your life do you think there's an opportunity to offer forgiveness and express generosity in a way that passes God's blessing along to another person?

Your memory

Psalm 107:1

Your action

- Identify the people in your life you would resist blessing and confess to God the reasons why.

- Make a list of ways to *water others' camels*.

CHAPTER FIVE

THE BLESSING:
God Blesses You Anyway

It's easy to find reasons not to bless. There's no fairness doctrine when it comes to blessings. God does not calculate blessings on a balance sheet where the blessings we receive correspond to the high quality of our character. God could find a thousand reasons to cut off blessings to us. But God blesses anyway.

God does not conduct a performance appraisal on the basis of our faithfulness and then reward us with blessings according to our output. Jesus said:

You have heard it said, "Love your neighbor and hate your enemy." But I say to you, "Love your enemy and pray for those who persecute you" so that you may be children of your Father in heaven; for He makes the sun rise on the evil and on the good and the rain to fall on the righteous and the unrighteous. For if you love those who love you, what reward do you have? Do not even the tax collectors do the same? And if you greet only your brothers and sisters, what more are you doing than others? Do not even the Gentiles do the same?

(Matthew 5:43-47)

Blessings defy expectation

An act becomes a blessing at exactly the point it becomes unfair—when it is better than the receiver deserves. Poor Jacob had managed to offend just about everyone. He'd deceived his father, fabricated a string of lies with his mother, and stolen his brother's most valued asset. He was hiding in the wilderness and utterly alone. It was exactly the life he deserved. And that's when God blessed him.

> *"Know that I am with you and will keep you wherever you go, and will bring you back to this land; for I will not leave you until I have done what I have promised you." Then Jacob woke from his sleep and said, "Surely the LORD is in this place—and I did not know it!" And he was afraid, and said, "How awesome is this place! This is none other than the house of God, and this is the gate of heaven."*
> (Genesis 28:15-17)

The next day, Jacob met his brother. He expected the worst, but Esau threw his arms around him and wept over him. And the blessings just kept on coming.

You lie—and God blesses anyway. You cheat—and God blesses anyway. You give into temptation—and God blesses anyway. You are arrogant, vindictive, cold-hearted, and selfish—and God blesses anyway. You are habitually and intentionally disobedient—and God blesses anyway.

Paul summarized it this way:

For while we were still weak, at the right time Christ died for the ungodly. Indeed, rarely will anyone die for a righteous person—though perhaps for a good person someone might actually dare to die. But God proves his love for us in that while we were still sinners Christ died for us.

(Romans 5:6-8)

This is not to say that God pays no mind to evil or that no consequences exist for our rebellious behavior. Nothing could be further from the truth. As the scriptures sternly warn, God will not be mocked (Galatians 6:7). But beyond the justice of God and within the consequences of our disobedience, God also blesses. In fact, the only thing that makes God's judgment tolerable are His blessings.

Even when we are at our worst, God blesses anyway. Even when we make bad choices that get us into trouble, God keeps marking our name on His trophy. Even when there is no good reason to do so, God blesses anyway.

CHAPTER SIX

THE APPLICATION:

Bless Others Anyway

People's bad behavior gives us plenty of reasons not to bless. E. Stanley Jones spent much of his career in India. He once wrote about a snake charmer who was having trouble with his poisonous cobra. It had become nasty and uncooperative. So he went to an expert on such things; the expert carefully uncoiled the cobra from its basket and then re-coiled it back in the opposite way. The snake had been coiled in its basket the wrong way. In a manner of speaking, most of the problems in the world come from people who are coiled wrong in their baskets. And when that's true, it's hard to think of blessing others. Bless them anyway.

Bless even when hurried, troubled, or distracted

Hurry is a frequent roadblock to blessing others. We've got places to go, things to do, and people to see. Our lives are often over-scripted. Opportunities to bless disappear behind the veil of our to-do lists and Post-It notes. Even if you're busy and only a third of the way down your to-do list, bless anyway.

Tragedies of life and other complicated circumstances make blessing others difficult. It's not that we're opposed to blessing others; in fact, under better conditions, we'd be the first to do so. But just not now. Bless anyway.

Distractions are a foil for blessing others. Woody Allen's answer to the question, "What do you believe in?" is provocative. "I believe," he said, "in the power of distraction." Perhaps more than at any other time in history, we are distracted. Bless anyway.

Our view of others gets in the way. They don't seem deserving. They have offended us. At the low point of Richard Nixon's presidency, he received a letter from Harold MacMilllan, the former Prime Minister of Great Britain, who wrote, "I feel compelled in view of our long friendship to send you a message of sympathy and good will. I trust that these clouds may soon roll away." After MacMilllan died, Nixon wrote a tribute in *The Times of London*, "What you learn when you fail is that you hear from your friends." Even if people seem unworthy of your blessings, bless them anyway.

Early in our marriage, Terri and I vacationed with family. We had no money, so staying with parents was a cheap vacation. But staying with parents didn't necessarily bring out the best in me back then. We were on our way to church and got into some kind of argument. It's not unusual for my default response to tension to be escape. So I stopped the car and got out. If you've ever considered this solution to an argument, I would recommend against it because figuring out what to do next is problematic. Of all the next-steps that came to mind, the only one that didn't further my embarrassment was to get back in the car. That's what I did. We drove in silence to the church, put the kids in child care, and went into the sanctuary. The service had already started. We squeezed into two seats in the back. A chill still remained between us. The pastor stood to read the morning scripture passage, and as God would have it on such an occasion, the text was this:

If I speak in the tongues of mortals and angels but have not love I am a noisy gong or a clanging cymbal...
Love is patient. Love is kind. Love is not jealous or boastful or arrogant or rude. Love does not insist on its own way.
It is not irritable or resentful.
(1 Corinthians 13:1, 4-5)

And as the pastor read, I felt my wife's hand reach over to rest on my arm. Despite the recent unhappiness between us, she blessed me anyway.

So this is the first step in the Bless Challenge. You have been made to receive God's blessings, and then, in turn, to bless others. As Paul put it:

Do all things without murmuring and arguing, so that you may be blameless and innocent, children of God without blemish in the midst of a crooked and perverse generation, in which you shine like stars in the world.

(Philippians 2:14-15)

There can be no greater blessing than to shine like stars in the world!

DIALOGUE BOX

Your journal

> Look back over your life and write about whether blessing others has seemed natural or unnatural to you.

Your prayers

> Ask God to bring to mind the people who most need you to bless them *anyway.*

Your discussion

> - What obstacles do you erect to receiving blessings from God?
>
> - Discuss some of the "conditions" you usually place on blessing others.

Your memory

> 1 Corinthians 13:4-7

Your action

> - Light a candle and give thanks for the way God blessed you when you were in a dark place.
>
> - Leave a simple gift for someone with whom you've recently had trouble.

PART TWO

SECTION ONE: LISTEN TO GOD
THROUGH THE WORLD GOD HAS MADE

God never stops talking. God is the supreme conversation-alist. The Bible tells us that creation got its start the moment God started talking. God speaks in two main languages—through the world He has made and through the Word He has spoken in the Bible. You are designed to receive person-alized messages from God's world and to receive messages from God's Word. The BLESS Challenge involves listening to God in the language of the world God has made and the Word God has spoken and then blessing others by what you hear.

Everything in creation speaks of God. Creation itself is a major player in the Bible record. After the flood, God re-set history and marked it with a **bow in the clouds**. Moses heard God speak from a **burning bush**. Israel needed de-liverance and God commissioned **gnats, frogs, flies, and locusts** as His agents. Israel looked for an escape route and the **seas pulled back their shores**. The Israelites needed a guide and were given a **cloud by day and a lightning storm**

at night. Elijah longed for a sign from God and found it in a **cloud.** People were hungry and **bread fell like dew from heaven**. Jesus' birth was marked by the appearance of a **star**, His death by an **eclipse** and an **earthquake**. When Jesus was told to keep His disciples quiet, He replied, *If these were quiet the **stones** themselves would cry out.*

> *The heavens are telling the glory of God and the firmaments proclaim His handiworks.*
> (Psalm 19:1)

Creation deserves an Academy Award for Best Supporting Actor.

The blessing of God-signs

You were made to listen to God and to hear Him through the world He has made. Years ago, my friend Jerry Kirk challenged me to assign some object with the responsibility for speaking to me and reminding me that God loves me and is intimately involved in my life. So I chose birds. This activity may sound silly or contrived, but even the Bible instructs us to find such reminders in creation.

> *But ask the animals, and they will teach you;*
> ***the birds of the air, and they will tell you;***
> *ask the plants of the earth, and they will teach you;*
> *and the fish of the sea will declare to you.*
> *Who among all these does not know that the hand of*
> *the LORD has done this?*

In his hand is the life of every living thing and the breath of
every human being.

(Job 12:7-10)

Every time I see a bird, I assume it was sent by God to remind me that God loves me and is involved in every detail of my life. And sure enough, the birds have appeared—everywhere.

I have also encouraged others to pick something. My daughter, Traci, chose the number 1111. Now this number appears everywhere in her life. After the doctor confirmed she was pregnant, at the next stop light, Traci noticed the temporary license plate on the car in front of her read 1111. She was so excited that she called and left a message on my phone. The time stamp on her message read 1111.

People tell me all sorts of things they've chosen as their God-sign. Butterflies, clouds, the wind, lost coins, pedestrians in crosswalks, red cars, rainbows, leaves, flowers. One girl told her dad, "I've chosen unicorns." Her dad said, "Why didn't you choose something more common?" She answered, "Dad, unicorns are everywhere." You see, if you assign something with the responsibility of revealing God's love for you, He will cause even the most obscure thing to show up in your life because God wants to bless you with the knowledge that He notices you.

Jane Trusty chose her cat, Pharaoh. Pharaoh was an outdoor cat, mostly wild. She chose him because he would disappear for long periods and then reappear to surprise her at unexpected moments—sort of like God. So she assigned Pharaoh the responsibility of reminding her of God's presence in her life. And then a strange thing happened. From then on, this previously aloof, here-today-and-gone-tomorrow cat never left her side. In the kitchen, he weaved between her legs. In the study, he sat on her lap. In the bedroom, he curled up on the bed. This four-legged feline creature spoke to Jane the deep mysteries of the presence of God.

God speaks to us personally through creation. In her Pulitzer Prize-winning book, *Pilgrim at Tinker Creek,* Annie Dillard tells how she listened to creation. After a year beside Tinker Creek in Virginia's Blue Ridge Mountains, she shared a dream that Ralph Waldo Emerson had: *"I dreamed that I floated at will in the great Ether, and I saw this world floating also not far off, but diminished to the size of an apple. Then an angel took it in his hand and brought it to me and said, 'This must thou eat.' And I ate the world."* If you truly want to listen to God, then swallow creation with your ears and eyes and hands. Embrace the world. Absorb the world. Adore the world. And if you do, God will add blessings on top of blessings through the world He has made.

CHAPTER ONE

THE BLESSING:
There's Hope for Tomorrow

When you listen to the world that God has made, it teaches you that God is endlessly creative. God knows nothing of dead-ends or impossibilities. There's always more. In the human body are 75-100 trillion cells. Each cell may have as many as 20,000 different types of protein, and of these, about 2,000 types will each be represented by at least 50,000 molecules; that means there may be as many as 100 million protein molecules in each cell.[1] Once again, this number is incomprehensible! Each cell has a unique assignment and each carries its own individual set of instructions for carrying out its work. You will never have to tell a cell what to do. Each cell is astonishingly complex and on average has about as many components as you would find in a Boeing 747.[2] For all we know about what's around us, it's estimated that it's only a fraction of all there is to know.

---

1 Bryson, Bill. *A Short History of Nearly Everything*, 378.
2 Ibid, 372.

We keep discovering more about the scale and scope of God's creation. At one time, we thought the earth was the center of everything. Then we thought it was the sun. Then we discovered the size of our solar system, and after that, the truly vast size of our Milky Way galaxy. For a long time, we thought that was it, but more recent discoveries lead us to believe there may be as many as 500 billion other galaxies. With every blink, we discover there's more.

Or take a simple block of forest soil, one foot square and one inch deep. In it you will find an average of 1,356 living creatures.[3] Most living creatures are small and easily overlooked. There are ten thousand bacteria in a spoonful of dirt. No one knows for sure, but experts speculate there are between 30 and 100 million species of insects and somewhere between 4,000 and 12,000 varieties of earthworms and 350,000 species of beetles. There are 250,000 varieties of plants and 2 billion tons of fish in the sea. And that's just today. Most of the creatures that have ever lived are not alive today. Ninety-nine percent of all the organisms that have ever existed since the dawn of time no longer exist.

There's always more in a blessing

Listen to God in the creative abundance of the world He has made and you will discover that God's operating principle is clearly this: There's more! And it has to do with far more

3 Brand, Paul and Philip Yancey. *Fearfully and Wonderfully Made: A Surgeon Looks at the Human and Spiritual Body*, 21.

than cells, proteins, bacteria, earthworms, and beetles. It has to do with life: More Life! And in this life there is more hope. More love. More power. More opportunity. More to be discovered. More ways through. More resources. More grace. God's creativity cannot be stopped. God's inventive imagination knows no limit.

This principle shows up everywhere. When God said to Abraham, *I will bless you and through you I will bless all the families of the earth,* there was just one impossible problem—Abraham's wife Sarah couldn't have children. How could God bless the future when there was no future for Abraham's bloodline? When Sarah overheard the announcement of her impending pregnancy, it seemed so outlandish that she laughed out loud. But nine months later, little Isaac was born. And Abraham and Sarah discovered that at the heart of God's blessings, there's always more!

When God said to Moses, *Tell Pharaoh, "Let my people go,"* all Moses could think was that the task was impossible. It would require confidence—and Moses had none. It would require authority—and Moses had none. It would require skill—and Moses had none. It would require power—and Moses had none. It would require a team—and Moses had none. But step-by-step, Moses discovered that for those who trust God, there is always much, much more!

When Elijah despaired, *I alone am left in Israel, God answered him, No Elijah, I have many people in this place. There's more!* (1 Kings 19:14-18)

Whenever the Israelites found themselves at a dead end and believed that God was finished with them—lifeless, faithless, leaderless, hopeless—a new day would dawn and the people would sing:

> *When the Lord restored the fortunes of Zion,*
> *we were like those who dream.*
> *Then our mouth was filled with laughter,*
> *and our tongue with shouts of joy;*
> *then it was said among the nations,*
> *"The Lord has done great things for them."*
> *The Lord has done great things for us,*
> *and we rejoiced.*
> (Psalm 126:1-3)

There's more!

People wept at Lazarus' tomb; the stench of death was everywhere. Jesus said, *Roll the stone away—Lazarus, come forth!* (John 11). And out he came—alive. There's more!

Jesus came to the home of the little girl who had died. He said, *She's only sleeping.* The people laughed and said, "We know death when we see it." But Jesus went in, took her by the hand and said, *Little girl, get up* (Mark 5). And immediately she got up. There's more!

They sealed Jesus' body in the grave and posted guards, but when the stone rolled away the tomb was empty. This moment was the exclamation point on Jesus' life. There's more!

Whenever Jesus connected with someone, He blessed that person by offering him or her the promise of something more. He forgave sinners, He healed the sick, He restored the lost, He fed the hungry, He gave hope to the hopeless, He raised the dead. There's more! Those words are what you hear when you listen to the world God has made.

All things connect to a blessing

When you listen to the world God has made, you also learn that everything is part of something else, and each one of us is part of all others. As Frederick Buechner puts it, creation is a spider web, and you can't touch any one part of it without shaking the whole. From the panorama of the Milky Way crawling across the night sky to the web of molecules that connect every human being to every human being, the world God created declares all things to be connected. I see the bumper sticker, "Practice random acts of kindness," but there are no random acts. Everything is connected. Listen to Bill Bryson's stunning summary of this:

> If your two parents hadn't bonded just when they did—possibly to the second, possibly to the nanosecond—you wouldn't be here. And if their parents hadn't bonded in a precisely timely manner, you wouldn't be here either.

And if their parents hadn't done likewise, and their parents before them, and so on, obviously and indefinitely, you wouldn't be here.[4]

Bryson presses this calculation back sixty-four generations to the time of the Romans and concludes that your existence depends on the perfectly timed cooperative efforts of 1,000,000,000,000,000,000 people. The math and science of this escapes me. The concept is fantastic. Your presence in the world is intimately connected to the timing of every other person's appearance in the world going back through ages and eons of history.

From a different angle, Bill Bryson goes on to offer this very odd and intriguing summary of the way DNA connects us to everything that exists. For example, scientists took the gene that controlled the development of a mouse's eye and inserted it into the larvae of a fruit fly. They had no idea what to expect, but expected something grotesque. In fact, the mouse-eye gene not only made a viable eye in the fruit fly, but it made a *fly's* eye. "Here were two creatures that hadn't shared a common ancestor for 500 million years, yet could swap genetic material as if they were sisters."[5] Researchers have discovered the same story wherever they look. Over 60 percent of human genes are fundamentally the same as those found in fruit flies. "Life, it appears, was drawn up

4 Bryson, Bill. *A Short History of Nearly Everything*, 397.
5 Ibid, 411.

from a single set of blue prints."[6] "Every living thing is an elaboration on a single original plan…Remarkably, we are even quite closely related to fruits and vegetables. About half the chemical functions that take place in a banana are fundamentally the same as the chemical functions that take place in you."[7]

Edward Lorenz was an American mathematician and meteorologist, and a pioneer of chaos theory. In the course of his research, he explored the world of cause and effect and coined the term *butterfly effect* that proposes that the movement of a butterfly's wings on one side of the world could so alter the atmosphere eventually leading to the formation of a hurricane on the other side of the world. The word God speaks through the world He has made tells us that everything is connected.

Two thousand years ago, St. Paul, the brilliant theologian, had already made this conclusion and determined that all things are connected in most remarkable ways. Jesus has His fingers on everything in creation. St. Paul wrote about Jesus:

He is the image of the invisible God, the first-born of creation;
for in Him all things in heaven and on earth were created,
things visible and invisible, whether thrones or dominions or
rulers or powers—all things have been created through Him
and for Him. He Himself is before all things and in Him all

6 Ibid, 412.
7 Ibid, 415.

things hold together.
(Colossians 1:15-17)

Every person and event is connected to every other person and event. Everything is charged with the question, "How will God use this in the greater drama of my life?"

Paul went on to announce:

We know that all things work together for good for those who love God, who are called according to His purpose.
(Romans 8:28)

Joseph, Abraham's great-grandson, had a strange blend of brilliance and arrogance that so angered his brothers that they sold him into slavery in Egypt. All alone, down in Egypt, things went from bad to worse for Joseph. But if you know the story, you remember how every piece got connected to every other piece so that in the end, Joseph's brothers found themselves asking for his help when Joseph had become a great leader in Egypt. Joseph declared to his terrified brothers:

Do not be afraid! Am I in the place of God? Even though you intended to do harm to Me, God intended it for good, in order to preserve a numerous people, as He is doing today.
(Genesis 50:19-20)

Everything is connected to a blessing and nothing is wasted.

CHAPTER TWO

THE APPLICATION:
Bless Others with Hope for Tomorrow

The world we live in can be profoundly discouraging. This world has a thousand ways to break your spirit. A recent popular television program, *Wipeout*, featured contestants navigating impossible obstacle courses of moving objects. Sooner or later, everyone falls in the mud. You wonder what can be so grandly entertaining about watching people fall in the mud? The producers say the show is popular simply because people like to watch other people fall down. Whenever a public figure "falls," it preempts all other news. When a friend, coworker, or neighbor falls, it's impossible to stop the buzz. We like to see people fall.

And the people around us are constantly failing and falling. Most of it is invisible to us and most of our disappointments we carry in disguise.

So it's not hard to imagine how it blesses someone to be on the receiving end of discovering that despite falling and failing, **there's more.**

Hope as a blessing

When you're down, it's hard to imagine yourself ever getting up. When you're sick, you can't ever imagine being well. A week after my mother retired, she was diagnosed with ovarian cancer; the retirement my parents had dreamt about turned into a sixteen-month nightmare of surgeries and treatments. After my mom died, my father fell into a black hole from which he feared he would never escape. But someone wrote him a note that said, "I've been where you are and I promise that you won't feel this way forever." And about a year later, my dad got up one morning and realized that for the first time in twelve months, for five minutes he felt happy. A few days later, he experienced ten minutes of happiness. And gradually, it spread out from there. That note became a lifeline of words that connected him to a better tomorrow.

Become bilingual in the lifestyle and language of hope and the behavior of encouragement. Sometimes, it will be a word you speak. Sometimes, it will be work that you do. Look for ways to translate God's vocabulary of hope into others' lives.

Within days of my sixteenth birthday, I became a licensed driver in the State of Oregon. We all know the euphoria of that great new day—driving down the avenue, one hand on the steering wheel, one elbow out the window, music playing, looking cool and in control. A week later, I had my first wreck. It was all my fault. I cornered too fast on a gravel road, panicked, hit the accelerator and not the brake, and buried the nose of the family's VW Beetle into a rock wall in front of my girlfriend's house. The car was towed home and dropped in the driveway. My dad circled the car, inspecting the damage—a crumpled fender, a mangled bumper, one headlight popped out and dangling from wires that made it look like a disembodied eyeball hanging on a nerve.

My father's icy silence convinced me I'd never drive again. So the next day, I was in the garage pumping up the tires on my bike. I had become a sixteen-year-old loser on a bike. That's when my dad stepped into the garage. He had something in his hand. When I held out mine, he dropped into it the keys to the family's other car. He said something about how when you fall off the horse, it's best to get back in the saddle right away. It took a moment for me to realize that those weren't just car keys; they were keys to a life where there's hope for tomorrow, a world where there's more.

You are surrounded by people who are thinking of giving up on tomorrow. In the movie *The Shawshank Redemption,* the old murderer named Red is paroled after thirty years in prison. It's true that he's a changed man, but after so long in prison, he doesn't know whether he can make it on the outside. As he puts it, "I've been institutionalized." He pauses in front of a pawn shop window. Inside is a shelf of compasses and a shelf of guns. He has to choose his future—a gun or a compass—despair or hope? Because of a promise made to him by another inmate that a better life lay just ahead, Red chose the compass.

It may be something that you do. It may be something that you say. It may be something that you give that helps others choose a compass and to believe there's more, there's hope, there's a blessing in tomorrow.

In recent years, I've had two brain surgeries to repair a rather unusual break in my temporal bone. After the first surgery failed, the second surgery was, by design, more invasive and dramatic. It involved the partial disabling and reconstruction of the balance system on my left side. When I awoke from surgery, my whole world was wildly whirling in circles. Imagine yourself in an enormous appliance store, surrounded 360 degrees from floor to ceiling with television screens all showing the same image. Now imagine that they all begin to rotate around you and there's nothing you can do to stop them. That was my world when I opened my eyes. It was horrifyingly disorienting. I thought I was going crazy. My family could see my eyes flipping wildly back-and-forth in their sockets. I lay there in ICU in my new insane, out-of-control world, thinking desperate thoughts. I wondered what I had done. A few days later, my neurosurgeon, Dr. Kim, while making his daily rounds, sat on the edge of my bed. I described to him my wretched condition. He examined me, asked a few questions, and asked whether together we could talk to my wife, Terri. So we telephoned her.

He declared to her in an authoritative voice, "Don't worry, Terri; he's golden." Frankly, at that moment I felt anything but golden, but Dr. Kim described an alternative future that was full of hope.

> *For surely I know the plans I have for you, says the Lord,*
> *plans for your welfare and not for harm,*
> *to give you a future with hope.*
> (Jeremiah 29:11)

God is the great conversationalist, and He's given you work to do and words to speak to continue what God has demonstrated so clearly in creation itself—There's more.

Pulling together the pieces of blessing

Everything is also part of something else. Sometimes, this connection can be bad. But when God is in it, even the worst things work together for good. As a thirteen-year-old, I lay on my bed fighting demons of worry. That's when my dad taught me my first life-altering scripture passage:

> *We know that all things work together for good for those who*
> *love God, who are called according to his purpose.*
> (Romans 8:28)

A thousand times since then, I've been rescued by that Divine principle. *All things work together for good....*Not just most things or the majority of things. Not generally speaking, or figuratively speaking. Not just the good things or the

important things. *ALL THINGS...WORK TOGETHER...
FOR GOOD!* All things are connected. Every event, no matter how bad or baffling, is a hyphenated form of goodness.

We've already mentioned the astonishing symbiosis of creation. God works the same principle in our daily lives. We bless others by helping them connect the apparently disconnected dots of their lives. All the triumphs and tragedies and traumas, the missteps and misfortunes and misadventures, all the expendable elements of ten thousand ordinary days—all these things are connected. The events in our lives don't end with a period; they end with a hyphen. Everything is part of something else.

A family vacationed in St. Vincent, Grenadines. The dad fell and ruptured his spleen. He nearly bled to death. A cabbie—a complete stranger—gave blood and the man survived. The dad asked, "Can I do anything to repay you?" The cabbie knew of some nuns at a nearby girl's school who had a student athlete who was very fast. She was, in fact, so fast that there was no real competition left for her on that tiny island. To run in more competitive meets required money to travel off the island. So, at the cabbie's request and out of gratitude, the man paid for her travel expenses. At one such track meet, the coach of the University of Iowa saw her run and recruited her to the university where she became a star athlete. A few years later, Kineke Alexander, this star athlete from the University of Iowa, carried the flag for St. Vincent, Grenadines into the Olympic Stadium representing her country. And that's how it came to be that a man who fell and nearly died, a cabbie with some extra blood to give, some nuns from a Catholic school, a promising young athlete, the coach of the University of Iowa, and the Olympic pride of a nation got connected. All this happened because people kept advancing a certain creative form of conversation.

Life's big moments are connected by the smaller moments, and God has given us the work of blessing to help others connect the dots. The journey toward goodness is a game of connect-the-dots. We bless people when we help them wonder how today's events will be used by God for some greater good tomorrow. How walking across the room and talking to a stranger might change the course of history. How taking a next step when you're tired, or you don't know where to go, will take you somewhere anyway. How hitting the reset button after personal failure can lead to a better tomorrow. How connecting people who don't yet know each other enriches each of their lives. This idea isn't just pie-in-the-sky. It's not just wishful thinking. It's not just whistling in the cemetery. It's the way the system we call life is made by God to work. It's the way God works in creation.

In his book, *The Hole in Our Gospel,* Richard Stearns refers to J. Wilbur Chapman's book *The Life and Work of Dwight Lyman Moody.* A remarkable string of events began with Edward Kimball, who was a faithful volunteer and teacher in the youth department of his church. One day, a young teenager attended his class. Kimball felt compelled to get to know the young man and visited him in the shoe store where he worked. He put his hand on his shoulder and rather awkwardly mentioned the love of Christ, and quite unexpectedly, the young man felt moved to commit his life to Christ. The young man's name was Dwight L. Moody, and he became the most impactful evangelist of the nineteenth century. Along the way, Moody played a part in the conversion of F.B. Meyer, who became a pastor and mentored J.W. Chapman, who became a pastor who started an outreach to professional baseball players. One of those players was Billy Sunday, who went on to become the greatest evangelist of the first half of the twentieth century. At one of Billy Sunday's crusades, Mordecai Ham came to Christ, and he in turn began an evangelistic outreach. At one of his crusades, a young man named Billy Graham came forward and offered his life to Christ. This whole string of history-changing events got started when Edward Kimball said a few words of blessing to a boy in a shoe shop.

Every person and every event is the link in a chain of events leading to a remarkable outcome that you cannot yet begin to fathom. The words God gives you to speak and the works God gives you to do are links in the chain to a better tomorrow for those around you. God speaks and creation unfolds. He is the supreme conversationalist. And by His design, the words we use continue His work of creation in blessing others' lives.

DIALOGUE BOX

Your journal

Write about an area of your life where you seem to be stuck at a dead end.

Your prayers

Ask God to help you understand some of the reasons why you are stuck at certain places of your life.

Your discussion

- In what kinds of situations have you discovered that people really need to know there is hope for a new beginning? Why?

- What areas of your life seem to be hanging like loose ends without resolution?

Your memory

John 1:5

Your action

- Pick something as your God-sign and ask God to use it to remind you of His love and presence.

- Who in your life needs a new beginning? Give a gift that would represent that to him or her.

SECTION TWO: LISTEN TO GOD
THROUGH THE WORD GOD SPEAKS

Creation declares the glory of God's creativity and abundance, but if you want the detail on God's character, if you want to understand His personality, if you want the specs on His design for human beings, and if you want to grasp His supernatural plan for an alternative future filled with hope, you need a book. You need the Bible. It is the Word God speaks.

I was once involved in a writing project on the literary works of Frederick Buechner. He's a Presbyterian pastor and so am I. It made sense that we should meet. So I wrote and proposed the conversation. He responded, "Everything I wish to reveal about myself I have written in my autobiographies. Sincerely, Frederick Buechner." This response was not the one I had hoped for or expected. It did occur to me, however, that God might say something like that about Himself. *Everything I wish to reveal about Myself I have written in My autobiography.* The only way to know God and His plan is to listen to what He says about Himself. Anything else is just guesswork.

When we say that God speaks through His Word, we must understand that the Bible itself identifies forty different authors writing across 1,500 years. Sometimes, God inspired an idea and allowed the writer to choose the forms and words. Sometimes, God spoke more directly as in the form of dictation. These authors wrote with widely ranging styles unique to them. Each writer received a blessing from God and passed that blessing along in words. Sometimes the authors wrote prose, sometimes poetry, sometimes history, sometimes prophecy, sometimes parable. Most did not collaborate. And yet the storyline from Genesis to Revelation forms history's most compelling, widely read, and revered document. This Word is ancient, but it's not old.

God's personalized Word of blessing

Toward the end of his life, my father gave me what remained of his library. Several of his books I already owned and others were of no particular interest to me. I did, however, pack a few of them in a box and ship them back to my home in Texas. My father died and the books sat in their box. A few months later, I noticed the box, opened it, and began to read the book on top, *A Diary of Readings*. A few pages in, I found a yellow sticky note with a message that read, "Dave, these readings have been a constant source of challenge and inspiration. Dad." A few pages later, I found another little yellow note, and then another. With that, I tore into the other books and found more notes—from my father. And gradually, it dawned on me that my father had left notes to me in his books. My father was speaking to me through his books. These books were alive with my father.

God wants to speak to you through His book. The Bible is a book full of personalized notes to you from your Heavenly Father. The Bible has been described as a box full of flashlights waiting to illuminate our darkness and a barrel full of time-bombs waiting to explode at just the right moments. There are 31,173 verses in the Bible. That's 31,173 flashlights and time bombs. Every day, thousands of flashes of light and perfectly timed explosions take place as people read these passages and God speaks with a force that rocks their lives.

CHAPTER ONE

THE BLESSING:
God's Word Breathes Life into You

I spent a few summers as a lifeguard on Lake Oswego in Oregon. To qualify required the usual swimming and life-saving certifications. Back then, the old back-pressure, arm-lift method was giving way to the newer mouth-to-mouth method. Unfortunately, there were no Resusci-Andys or Resusci-Annies to learn on. We learned on each other—boys-on-boys and girls-on-girls. With only a piece of gauze between us, we took turns breathing into each other. Once I adjusted to the creepiness factor of a male classmate breathing into me, I couldn't ignore the fascinating sensation of my own lungs filling with another's breath. Can there be anything more personal than a person's own breath? Your breath carries the scent of you. Your breath carries the warmth of you.

God's Word says:

> *All scripture is inspired by God.*
> (2 Timothy 3:16)

The biblical words for *spirit* and *breath* are interchangeable. That means that to be *God-inspired* is to be *God-breathed.* God's Word is as personal to Him as His own breath. When the Bible says it is God-breathed, it means the Bible is deeply personal. It means it carries God's scent and God's warmth. The Word of God is alive with the very essence of God. The Words of God in the Bible breathe God's own Being into you.

Years ago, I decided to take seriously memorizing God's Word. I started small with short verses I'd write on the back of friends' business cards and carry in the car. I'd repeat them while driving back and forth. Then I tried longer sections—Psalms and chapters. Then eventually, some whole books of the Bible. Along the way, I discovered that memory is not a gift; it is a discipline. Memorization is simply sustained repetition. To retain the verses I'd memorize meant I'd have to repeat them over and over. Finding time to repeat them required reassigning my mind to different tasks. The more I memorized, the more I had to find time to repeat what I had memorized. It started in the car. In the car I had my Monday cards and my Tuesday cards, my Wednesday cards—a stack of cards for every day of the week. Instead of listening to the news or music or shaking my fist at idiot drivers, I let God breathe His ideas into my mind. But it wasn't long before car-time wasn't enough time for all I had to remember. So over time, I have reassigned what I do with my mind while I'm showering, while I'm shaving, while I'm on the treadmill, when I'm buttering my toast, when I lay in my bed, when I rise up in the morning. It is what I do with many hours of my life—I remember. To you, this process may sound tedious and confining, but to me, it's been liberating. My thoughts are always setting off on questionable journeys—into regions of fear, anxiety, old wounds, nursed hurts, petty feuds, insecurities, temptations, and desires. But by regularly choosing to think God's Word, instead I receive CPR for my mind. God's Word breathes blessings into me.

When I had brain surgery to repair a rather rare unusual break in my temporal bone, I awoke from surgery to find my whole world was wildly whirling in circles. As I lay there alone in the ICU in my insane, out-of-control world, I began thinking desperate thoughts. I wondered what I had done. I thought to myself, "If I have to live this way, I will kill myself." I was desperate! But then I remembered:

> *The thought of my affliction and my*
> *homelessness is wormwood and gall!*
> *My soul continually thinks of it and*
> *is bowed down within me.*
> *But this I call to mind, and therefore I have hope:*
>
> *The steadfast love of the Lord never ceases,*
> *His mercies never come to an end;*
>
> *They are new every morning.*
> *great is your faithfulness.*
> (Lamentation 3:19-21)

Those words were CPR for my terrified mind. They were a lifeline to God's alternative future.

When fear sends you running for cover, God's Word breathes the blessing:

God did not give us a spirit of cowardice, but rather a spirit of power and of love and of self-discipline.

(2 Timothy 1:4)

When guilt scolds and shame ridicules, God's Word breathes the blessing:

The Lord is merciful and gracious,
slow to anger and abounding in steadfast love.

He will not always accuse,
nor will he keep his anger forever.
He does not deal with us according to our sins,
nor repay us according to our iniquities.
For as the heavens are high above the earth,
so great is his steadfast love towards those who fear him;
as far as the east is from the west,
so far he removes our transgressions from us.
As a father has compassion for his children,
so the Lord has compassion for those who fear him.
For he knows how we were made;
he remembers that we are dust.

(Psalm 103:8-14)

When confusion paralyzes and uncertainty rules, God's Word breathes the blessing:

For surely I know the plans I have for you, says the Lord,
plans for your welfare and not for harm,
to give you a future with hope.
(Jeremiah 29:11)

When either you have moved from God or God has moved from you and you feel abandoned and alone, God's Word breathes the blessing:

"Surely the Lord is in this place—and I did not know it!"
And he was afraid, and said, "How awesome is this place!
This is none other than the house of God,
and this is the gate of heaven."
(Genesis 28:16-17)

When you are weak and broken down by life, God's Word breathes the blessing:

Have you not known? Have you not heard?
The Lord is the everlasting God,
the Creator of the ends of the earth.
He does not faint or grow weary;
his understanding is unsearchable.
He gives power to the faint,
and strengthens the powerless.

Even youths will faint and be weary,
and the young will fall exhausted;
but those who wait for the Lord shall renew their strength,
they shall mount up with wings like eagles,
they shall run and not be weary,
they shall walk and not faint.
(Isaiah 40:28-31)

When sickness engulfs you and you can't imagine being well, God's Word breathes the blessing:

Bless the Lord, O my soul,
and all that is within me,
bless his holy name.
Bless the Lord, O my soul,
and do not forget all his benefits—
who forgives all your iniquity,
who heals all your diseases,
who redeems your life from the Pit,
who crowns you with steadfast love and mercy,
who satisfies you with good as long as you live
so that your youth is renewed like the eagle's.
(Psalm 103:1-5)

When death comes knocking, God's Word breathes the blessing:

I am the resurrection and the life. Those who believe in me,
even though they die, will live, and everyone who lives and

believes in me will never die.
(John 11:25-26)

God's Word blesses by teaching

Any life that you invent for yourself will be inferior and fatally flawed. Your best life is not a life you can think up for yourself. It is a life that we must be taught. The Bible is... *useful for teaching.*

Remember that I said people think somewhere around 12,000 to 30,000 thoughts a day. The mind is like popcorn with thoughts exploding and ricocheting in every direction. These thoughts carry us from the lofty to the lowly, from the noble to the grotesque. The route to a transformed life must pass through the territory of what you think about. The natural course of our thoughts declares one kind of life and one kind of future. The supernatural course of God's thoughts declares an alternative authentic life and a better future. The difference in your life is determined by which curriculum you study.

Keep in mind that every person who ever lived started out as a blank slate. At birth, none of us can tell a beach ball from a 747. We can't distinguish Bach from the Beatles or a carrot from a corkscrew. We come into this world as a blank slate with staggering potential, and the difference between the blank slate and the realized potential is almost always a teacher.

Everything that happens in life is made possible by instruction. The cars we drive, the roads that carry them, the neighborhoods they connect exist because someone taught someone. The plans we make and the paths we follow exist because someone taught someone.

It's hard to overstate the implications of this truth. It's likely that the main difference between Mother Teresa and Adolph Hitler was a teacher. In a compact sense, the teacher announces and demonstrates what something is before it can be clearly seen by the student. Sometimes, this announcement is accompanied by words, sometimes not.

One Sunday afternoon when we were vacationing in Mexico, I took a break from the heat to watch a golf tournament on TV. There was an intriguing technical difficulty. The picture was delayed three-seconds behind the sound. That meant you heard before you saw. The announcer described drives, chips, and putts before they were actually seen. The crowd groaned and cheered before you could see why. The broadcaster was a kind of teacher announcing what was to come. That's the way God's Word works. It announces reality before it can be seen, and your response to the instruction determines which reality you experience. Being taught by God's Word blesses you and surrounds your life with boundaries of hope.

God's Word blesses by teaching. God's Word reveals a design that cannot be otherwise known. We do not always find this Word to be agreeable. Sometimes, it is confusing. Sometimes, it runs contrary to popular thought. Sometimes, it demands what seems impossible. Even so, it is the way life works. It is God's announcement of the alternative future that blesses because it works.

God's Word blesses by correcting and reproving

God made you according to certain specifications. The United States Government issues black pens that you see everywhere in government offices. The National Industries for the Blind produces 75,000 of these pens a day at $6.92/ dozen according to a sixteen-page book of specifications. The pen must write continuously the distance of a mile without skipping or blobbing, in temperatures ranging from 40 below to 160 above. The ink must remain visible on paper even after forty-eight hours submerged in water, or two applications of chemical bleach. The black barrel of the pen must be the length of 150 miles on the official U.S. navy maps, be corrosion resistant, and not warp or crack or fade. It must burn at the rate of 2.5 inches/minute so as to be useful as a fuse. These are its specifications.

You also have been made according to specifications that are described in the Bible. But the world has its own specifications that seem appealing, logical, and compelling. The chief task in life involves choosing your specifications.

*Do not be conformed to this world, but be transformed by
the renewing of your minds, so that you may discern what is
the will of God—what is good and acceptable and perfect.*
(Romans 12:2)

This choice is intensely difficult. As the Bible puts it:

*I do not understand my own actions. For I do not do what I
want, but I do the very thing I hate…For I delight in the law
of God in my inmost self, but I see in my members another
law at war with the law of my mind, making me captive to
the law of sin that dwells in my members…So then, with my
mind I am a slave to the law of God, but with my flesh I am a
slave to the law of sin.*
(Romans 7:15-25)

Every person experiences the frustration of competing
impulses every day. We drift. Remember again that when
Woody Allen was asked what he believed in, he answered,
"I believe in the power of distraction." And that's the truth.

We wander this way and that and need a lot of what the
Bible describes as correction and reproof. The situation re-
minds me of something I heard years ago about the Apollo
missions to the moon. A researcher discovered that the
Voyager was off course something like 83 percent of the time.
A friend who worked for NASA at the time explained that
the *Voyager* was able to carry only a very limited amount of
fuel, much of which was needed to launch from the moon's

surface. So for most of the 700,000 mile journey to the moon and back, the *Voyager* drifted. And without power for guidance, the *Voyager* invariably drifted off course. So, at certain predetermined locations, the retro-rockets were fired to put the *Voyager* back on course. The journey to the moon was not a straight line but a meandering course.

The human journey is also a meandering course. Allowing God's Word to teach us continually draws us back to the right course.

A few miles above Niagara Falls, the Niagara River flows with lazy currents. But a danger of catastrophic proportions is just downstream. I understand that a few miles upstream, stretched across a lazy section of the river, tow cables have been stretched. From the first, a hanging sign asks, "Do you have an anchor?" And from the second, a hanging sign asks, "Do you know how to use it?"

God knows the dangerous currents that pull on our lives. God's Word is an anchor to ground and to correct our course in the dangerous currents of life.

God's Word blesses by training in righteousness

We are made by God for relationships. The first not-good thing in the Bible is aloneness (Genesis 2:18). And yet, even though we are made for relationships, relationships are not natural to us. As the old saying goes, we are like porcupines in winter; we need each other's warmth, but our quills keep driving us apart. Broken relationships are the central problem of the human race. Healthy relationships are life's greatest blessing. As the saying goes, no amount of success can make you happy if your relationships are broken, and no amount of failure can undo your happiness if your relationships are strong.

God's main occupation in history is the care and feeding of relationships. The Bible calls it *training in righteousness* (2 Timothy 3:17). The Bible is God's unparalleled training manual for relationships.

Were it not for relationships, there would be no story to tell. Were it not for relationships, there would be no need for language, no reason for families, no value in community. Bookstores would close; authors would go mute. Hollywood would wither away. There would be no email or Twitter, Facebook, or LinkedIn, no talk shows, newspapers, or magazines. Without relationships, the "social" would go out of social-networking—and so would the "net."

Relationships are our most fundamental reality, and yet we devote alarmingly little time to teaching them. By the time we reach twenty, we've received years of instruction in math, the sciences, reading, history, the arts, geography, government, and languages. To advance from grade level to grade level, we've got to demonstrate proficiency in all these skills, but when it comes to the complexity of establishing, caring for, and repairing the fundamental and foundational activity of our lives—our relationships—we're mostly left on our own.

If we're lucky, we come from families and a neighborhood where pursuing healthy relationships is a constant spoken and unspoken goal. But even then, the outcomes are never perfect. The problem is that we are not perfect. At our core, we are inwardly-absorbed and relationships require us to be outwardly-focused. The Word God speaks is all about reversing the natural instinct and flow of human nature from inward-absorption to outward-focus.

On this point, God's Word is the masterwork. All of the books that have ever been written on the subject of relationships are simply footnotes when compared to the magnum opus of scripture. It is impossible to quantify all that we would not know about the care and feeding of relationships if God's Word had not been written.

Without God's Word, we would be deprived of the Ten Commandments, which are the foundation stones of human behavior.

Without God's Word, we would not know that keeping these commandments is the only sure way to love others.

Without God's Word, we would not understand that loving others by keeping God's Commandments requires dying to self.

Without God's Word, we would not understand that the ability to love others by dying to self is a gift we receive from God, and the power to love as we have been loved comes from God's Spirit working within us.

Without God's Word, we would not know:

If I speak in the tongues of mortals and of angels, but do not have love, I am a noisy gong or a clanging cymbal. And if I have prophetic powers, and understand all mysteries and all knowledge, and if I have all faith, so as to remove mountains, but do not have love, I am nothing. If I give away all my possessions, and if I hand over my body so that I may boast, but do not have love, I gain nothing.

Love is patient; love is kind; love is not envious or boastful or arrogant or rude. It does not insist on its own way; it is not irritable or resentful; it does not rejoice in wrongdoing, but rejoices in the truth. It bears all things, believes all things, hopes all things, endures all things.

Love never ends. But as for prophecies, they will come to an end; as for tongues, they will cease; as for knowledge, it will come to an end. For we know only in part, and we prophesy only in part; but when the complete comes, the partial will come to an end. When I was a child, I spoke like a child, I thought like a child, I reasoned like a child; when I became an adult, I put an end to childish ways. For now we see in a mirror, dimly, but then we will see face to face. Now I know only in part; then I will know fully, even as I have been fully known. And now faith, hope, and love abide, these three; and the greatest of these is love.

(1 Corinthians 13)

The Biltmore Estate in Asheville, North Carolina is one of America's great homes. It was built in the late 1800s by George Washington Vanderbilt. It sits on 8,000 acres, has 175,000 square feet and 250 rooms. The manner of its construction and the history contained within its walls are layers and layers deep. Thousands visit there. When you arrive, you have two choices—take a self-guided tour or rent the headset that tells the story of each room's construction and the events that have taken place there. The headset comes with various settings that give access to layers and layers of detail. Some people are in a hurry and some people don't want to spend the money, so they don't invest in the headset. They see what they see and decide what they decide, but they learn little of the facts. After an hour or so, they walk back to the parking lot, shrug, smile, and say, "Nice house." But the people who invest in the headsets and hear the stories find themselves absorbed into the tissue and breadth of the house. It's no longer stone and wood, walls and windows; the house itself breathes its life on them.

When it comes to *training in righteousness,* God's Word is the headset; without it, we are left to invent for ourselves the definition and demands of the most complex and essential element of human life.

CHAPTER TWO

THE APPLICATION:
Breathe Life into Others

Four months after the 2010 earthquake that devastated Haiti, I traveled there. Conditions remained worse than grim. The only signs of hope came from organizations like Haiti Outreach Ministries. Its founder, Pastor Leon Dorleans, asked me to speak to his men's group. His topic surprised me—how to keep your wife happy. With unemployment at 80 percent, a non-functioning government, a life expectancy of fifty-three years in the poorest country in the Western Hemisphere, crippled by an horrific earthquake, life still came down to this—how to keep your wife happy. So I set about to teach on manhood from a biblical perspective. About 150 men were in the room and lots of noise outside. Since my voice isn't strong and I didn't have a microphone, I instinctively asked, "Can you hear me in the back?" And then it occurred to me that the question made no sense since I only speak English and they understood only French and Creole. As it turned out, the only person in the room who really needed to hear me was Pastor Leon because he was my translator. As long as he was close enough to hear me, that's all that mattered. And you are the translator of God's blessings to others. Stay close enough to hear His voice and then translate it into the life you live:

> *Through those who are near me I will show myself holy, and*
> *before all the people I will be glorified.*
> (Leviticus 10:3)

When you stay close enough to God for Him to breathe His blessings into you, you become a blessing to others.

Bless others by teaching

My brother-in-law, Dave Rock, is an artist. To be more precise, he's a muralist whose works can be found all over the world. Terri and I sat on barrels set on scaffolding in Chicago's Shedd Aquarium while watching him paint a jungle out of a blank wall. I asked, "How do you do that? What's the secret of painting?" He answered simply, "It's just a matter of putting the right color in the right place." In every aspect of life, we all want and need to know how to put the right color in the right place. The people who help us are those with knowledge and experience in the field. They are our teachers.

Of course, I'm referring to more than a classical education from a certified teacher in an accredited institution of learning. That's also essential, but life depends on being street smart as well as school smart, and that requires an education in every area of life.

One of life's most sobering truths is that everyone is a teacher to someone. And you don't have to have a Ph.D., multiple degrees, certifications, or even a classroom to teach. Your life gives instruction to someone. The question is: What kind? When God gets into you, He wants to rub off of you and onto those around you. Your life becomes your classroom and God's work in you becomes your curriculum.

Your main work in blessing others is to teach them about God's alternative life and His better future.

For twenty-eight years, Woody Hayes coached at Ohio State University, winning three National Collegiate Championships. He was known for winning games and losing his temper. His outstanding career disintegrated after the 1978 Gator Bowl. With the game on the line, Charlie Bauman, a player for Clemson, intercepted a pass and was run out of bounds on the Ohio State sideline. After the play was over, Coach Hayes stepped onto the field and punched Bauman in the throat. The next day, Coach Hayes was fired. He retired in humiliation. A few weeks later, a prestigious gathering of coaches and athletes from across the country was held. Tom Landry, the acclaimed coach of the Dallas Cowboys, had an extra ticket. He invited the humiliated and discredited former coach, Woody Hayes, as his guest. When they walked together into the banquet hall and the heads all started to turn, in that moment, Coach Landry became Professor Landry—a teacher of grace and mercy.

All of God's blessings are accompanied with a teaching certificate. When God forgives you, He equips you to become a teacher of forgiveness. When God pours generosity and kindness into your life, He qualifies you to become a professor of kindness and generosity. When God is patient and long-suffering toward you, He sends you out to personify patience and long-suffering. When God strengthens you to overcome affliction, He commissions you as a case study in perseverance.

God designed you to teach others. God's Word at work in your life is your lesson plan. Every teacher needs a lesson plan. The Bible is God's lesson plan. As the old saying goes, people are entitled to their own opinions, but not their own facts. God's Word contains the facts. Become familiar with the facts. Let them teach you what you know.

Decide what you know about love—that it is a gift from God, and that you cannot know how to love unless you know God's love—that love is outwardly focused, does not insist on its own way, and never gives up.

Decide what you know about forgiveness—that it is a gift from God, and that the failure to forgive makes a better future impossible; it imprisons the one who needs to forgive even more than the one who needs to be forgiven.

Decide what you know about sin—that it is the refusal to trust God's love, and that it enslaves a person.

Decide what you know about evil—that it is the distortion of something good; that it is subtle and disguises itself as 10,000 pretty-good things. That it is fundamentally self-destructive.

Decide what you know about human suffering—that God's ultimate plan is freedom from suffering. But even though suffering is not God's ultimate plan for humanity, He uses it for good by insuring that His *light shines in the darkness and the darkness cannot put it out.*

Decide what you know about God's will—that it is narrow with respect to character. We have been made according to specifications of holiness. But when our character follows God's design, God's will for us becomes broad with respect to the many decisions we make.

Decide what you know about Jesus—that He is what God looks like in human flesh and what people are supposed to look like in everyday life. That He alone is God's perfect solution to the problem of sin.

Decide what you know about heaven—that anyone who wants to go there gets to, as long as that person is willing to live according to God's design.

In 2011, Margaret Martin received the Presidential Citizenship Award for her creation of the Harmony Project. The idea is to turn hard times into harmony. She started in 2001 with thirty-six kids; by 2011, she had 1,500 children in the program. Each child is given a free instrument and tutoring as long as he or she stays in school. The program is turning countless kids' lives around and helping them to choose a better future. Margaret's own life required a turn-around. She was trapped in an abusive marriage, but, eventually, she escaped with her children, living for a time in poverty in an empty office building. Margaret went back to school and earned a Ph.D. in public health. But the real turning point came on the day when she watched her young son playing his violin in a farmer's market. A group of gang members gathered around him and were transfixed by his music. And gradually, they began to put money into his violin case. That's when Margaret Miller realized that they would rather do what he was doing than what they were do-ing, if only they had a chance.

For a moment, her little boy was teacher, and his lesson plan was a blessing. The world is starving for people who bless by teaching truth. Some teach with words and some teach with works. People of every age and stage of life teach and need teachers, from the polished and professional to the rough-cut and street wise, from the official and certified, to the unofficial and amateur. The world is changed and blessed by teachers. Listening to God gives us a curriculum and a con-nection to the classrooms of life.

Bless others by correcting and reproving

We are designed by God to bless others by correcting and reproving them. We bless others by giving them boosts in the right direction. God corrects and reproves us to keep us on course. Even though it may not always feel like it at the time, correction is an important component of God's blessing, and it's a part of God's blessing we are designed to pass on to others. This instruction is, of course, a very delicate matter. The best tools for keeping life on course are an equal blend of conviction and compassion. Followers of Jesus are people of conviction and compassion. People who bless others are those who believe strongly in the Jesus-life, but they apply their belief with a skilled touch. Too much conviction makes us brittle and unapproachable. Too much compassion makes us permissive and unprincipled. The extremes always leave wounds.

To bless others requires that you blend equal quantities of conviction and compassion. Sometimes, this form of blessing means we present people with the straightforward truth of biblical conviction. Sometimes, it means we demonstrate the warmth of biblical compassion. Usually, it means we do both.

The Bible captures this balance when it teaches us to:

> ...*speak the truth in love.*
> (Ephesians 4:15)

On that day when, as a sixteen-year-old, I drove like an idiot and wrecked the family Volkswagen, after surveying the damage to the car—the crumbled fender, the driver-side headlight dangling like an eyeball hanging by a nerve—my father walked slowly by me. As he passed, he kicked me in the rear. It was a kind of soccer-style kick, and it was clearly not designed to wound, but rather to express displeasure. And then in the next moment, he threw his arms around me in a gracious hug. It was my dad's way of expressing conviction and compassion. In that moment, I received a double blessing of my father's conviction and compassion.

In the first year of my ministry, serving a small church in the tiny farming town of Reardan, Washington, it was reported to me that the word on the street was that I was "stuck up." I was horrified. Stuck up? Shy, yes. Reserved, yes. Awkward around people, yes. But stuck up, no! It was my awkwardness around people that gave the wrong impression. The day I heard that, I began to work on changing the public presentation of myself. Forty years later, I remain that reserved person, but I've worked hard to correct any misimpression that might come from that. And I owe the changes in behavior to the courageous friend who *spoke the truth in love* to me.

When I arrived as the new pastor of the First Presbyterian Church of Spokane, Washington, Dale Bruner, renowned New Testament Professor and Bible teacher, taught a class to 400 adults between worship services. He invited questions at the end of each class. After I'd been there a month or two, someone asked, "Dr. Bruner, what do you think of our new pastor?" He paused and then answered, "Well, I like him—but there is one thing that bothers me; when he finishes reading the scripture passage, he lays the Bible on the Communion Table and walks away." Sitting in the balcony, I wanted to disappear. Mostly because what he said was the truth. I did spend too much time telling stories and not enough time engaging the Bible. From that day on, I've never put the Bible aside, neither when preparing to speak nor when I speak. Dale and his remarkable wife, Kathy, have become dear friends, and my life and work have been dramatically blessed by my friend who *spoke the truth in love* and *corrected and reproved me.*

One day, our car slid down an icy hill and hit a curb at the bottom. It didn't look like any damage had been done until we tried to drive the car again. Then, something was seriously wrong with the steering. The mechanic tried and tried but finally announced, "That is as good as I can make it." And from then on, the car pulled firmly toward the right. Driving that car required a firm hand on the wheel to keep it out of the ditch. So does life. Blessed is the life that is regularly *corrected and reproved.* Without the blessing of help from others, everyone's headed for the ditch. With conviction and compassion, bless others with *correction and reproof.*

Bless others by training in righteousness

Go online or to the library or to a bookstore, if you can find one these days, and count the number of books on relationships. Dr. Phil, Oprah Winfrey, Dr. Laura, and 100,000 therapists move like explorers through the thickets, swamps, and wilderness of relationships. Why? Because relationships are hard.

As I said, the Bible is God's brilliant sourcebook on relationships. From cover-to-cover it's about the impact of broken relationships and the care, feeding, and repair of relationships. At one point, the Bible offers this advice:

> *As God's chosen ones, holy and beloved, **clothe yourselves** with compassion, kindness, humility, meekness, and patience. Bear with one another and, if anyone has a complaint against another, forgive each other; just as the Lord has forgiven you, so you also must forgive. Above all, clothe yourselves with love, which binds everything together in perfect harmony.*
> (Colossians 3:12-14)

Three days a week, I try to spend time at the local fitness center. I can tell you that the men's locker room is not a pretty place. And the issue isn't the space; it's the men who fill it. I can't speak for women, but I can for men—clothes are one of the greatest contributions ever devised for men. Even in a fitness center where everyone is doing his best to take care of his physical body, the sights can be alarming. As for me, I avoid mirrors at all costs. The truth is, after the age of six or seven, people look so much better with their clothes on! God seems to acknowledge this fact when He teaches us—*clothe yourself*. Don't let the world see the naked truth about you. Frankly, I'd be mortified for people to know what I'm really thinking and feeling sometimes. It's personally humiliating to realize how petty, how critical, how depraved, how frightened, how resentful, how devious, how conniving, how judgmental, how self-absorbed I can actually be. The only thing that saves me socially is that I clothe my inner ugliness with the outer wardrobe of *compassion, kindness, humility, meekness, patience, forbearance, forgiveness, and love.*

Years ago, the popular TV program *The Twilight Zone* featured the story of a man who found a pair of eyeglasses that, when he wore them, allowed him to know what other people were really thinking by reading their private thoughts. Sometimes, what he saw was funny, sometimes touching, but mostly it was pretty ugly. At the close of the segment, the man stood in front of a mirror, and with trembling hands, he slid the eyeglasses into place to see the truth about himself. I can't remember exactly what he saw, but I do remember the sound of his horrified scream. Ironically, a short time later, I came upon a pair of eyeglasses that were identical to the ones in that TV show. With trembling hands, I stood in front of a mirror wondering what I would see. But I didn't have the courage to put them on for fear of seeing the truth about myself.

Two truths are at work in us. The first is that the world is better off not to see us exactly as we are. I suppose this statement may seem phony. We may assume that unless we are naturally and authentically good, pretending to be so by dressing up is deceitful. But if we wait to leave our room until all our motives are pure, we will live an isolated existence. That's why it's so kind of God to give us a wardrobe we can wear that makes us suitable and presentable for life in this world.

The second truth is that in most of us, perhaps all of us, is a deep yearning to present a better self to the world—to be compassionate, kind, humble, meek, patient, and loving. Putting on these behaviors, as the Bible instructs, is more than pretend; it's living the life we were meant to live.

God knows that although we are plagued by an inward ugliness that makes us unfit for life, another side of us truly and deeply wants to connect with people in ways that bless and heal. So God supplies us with these clothes to wear—with behaviors to "put on"— to present the better side of our character to the world until that day when our inner transformation into the likeness of Christ is made complete. St. Francis captured some of the intent of this desire in his classic prayer:

Lord, make me an instrument of your peace.

Where there is hatred, let me sow love.

Where there is injury, pardon.

Where there is doubt, faith.

Where there is despair, hope.

Where there is darkness, light.

Where there is sadness, joy.

O Divine Master,

grant that I may not so much seek to be consoled, as to console;

to be understood, as to understand;

to be loved, as to love.

For it is in giving that we receive.

It is in pardoning that we are pardoned,

and it is in dying that we are born to Eternal Life.

Amen.

Choosing God's designer-wear for relationships will always require one fundamental action—die to self. I said in the beginning that I could summarize all 31,173 verses in the Bible in one verse—*You are blessed by God to bless others.* Now I can summarize the secret of relationships with one phrase—die a little to live a lot.

Jesus puts it this way:

If any want to become my followers, let them deny themselves and take up their cross daily and follow me. For those who want to save their life will lose it, and those who lose their life for my sake will save it.

(Luke 9:23-24)

This act of dying to self sounds lethal, but it turns out to be life-giving. Dying to self resurrects relationships. As Paul put it:

> *I appeal to you, therefore, brothers and sisters, by the mercies of God, to present your bodies as a living sacrifice, holy and acceptable to God, which is your spiritual worship.*
> (Romans 12:1)

Dying to self doesn't kill you. The only sacrifice the Bible knows is a living sacrifice.

Lauren Freeman, a local TV news anchor, went on maternity leave. The first day back on-air, the small-talk included all the predictable questions and ribbing about motherhood. After a while, Lauren said something like, You know, before my baby was born, everyone told me about how I could kiss my old life goodbye. People went on and on about sleepless nights and dirty diapers, barf and boogers, but the one thing no one told me, the one thing I wasn't prepared for, was that I didn't mind. No one prepared me for how worth it it would be to lose my life for the sake of my child.

> *No one has greater love than this, to lay down one's life for one's friends.*
> (John 15:13)

It happens a hundred ways:

Every act of forgiveness requires a small death to self.

Every act of generosity requires a small death to self.

Every act of compassion requires a small death to self.

Every act of kindness requires a small death to self.

Every act of patience requires a small death to self.

Every act of humility requires a small death to self.

Every act of love requires a small death to self.

And when living this way, the miraculous discovery is that you haven't lost your life, you've gained it, and so have others.

In more than forty years of marriage, it has become very clear that my wife Terri is global in her thinking while I am focused. I mean that she can manage many thoughts and activities at one time, but I tend to be good for only one thing at a time. This quality makes her wonderfully flexible and me maddeningly focused. Sometimes, this difference of disposition shows up at bedtime. For me, preparing for bed is like shutting down a computer. I log out of all the programs I've opened during the day. Then my mental computer asks whether I really want to shut down; I push "shut down," pull up the sheets, turn off my light, close my eyes, and focus on the task at hand—going to sleep! Terri, on the other hand, has the capacity to keep all of her programs open all the time. She never shuts down. So when she gets in bed, her radar continues to hum like NORAD. It's not unusual for her to ask, out of the blue, with the lights off and the sheets pulled up, whether I've spoken to so-and-so, or remembered to do such-and-such. For me to respond requires that I turn on my computer, sign in with my password, and open up my operating systems and programs. I wish I could say I handle this difference with good cheer. But because I would prefer that she wait until morning when my computer is up and running to ask these questions, my response with the lights off and the sheets pulled up is, sadly, less than loving. But somewhere inside me, I know that for our relationship to be the best it can be, I need to die to myself and my own needs and interests, and on the occasions when I actually do that—when I die to myself just a little—we live better.

...

Any life you make up for yourself is destined for futility. It has little power to bless you or others. But when you listen to God through the astonishing world that He has made and in the incomparable Word that He has spoken, the blessings begin to flow.

DIALOGUE BOX

Your journal

When have you felt closest to God? Most distant?

Your prayers

> *Breathe on me, Breath of God, Fill me with life anew,*
> *That I may love what Thou dost love,*
> *And do what Thou wouldst do.*

> *Breathe on me, breath of God, Fill me with life anew,*
> *That I may love what Thou dost love,*
> *And do what Thou wouldst do.*

> *Breathe on me, breath of God, Until my heart is pure,*
> *Until with Thee I will one will, To do and to endure.*

> *Breathe on me, breath of God, Till I am wholly Thine,*
> *Until this earthly part of me, Glows with Thy fire divine.*

> *Breathe on me, breath of God, So shall I never die,*
> *But live with Thee the perfect life, Of Thine eternity.*

— Edwin Hatch and Robert Jackson

Your discussion

- What role has the Bible played in your life?

- In what ways have your life-experience and what you have learned in the Bible prepared you to teach others?

Your memory

2 Timothy 3:16-17

Your action

- Write a letter to someone you love expressing your affection and hopes for him or her.

- Write brief scripture passages on the back of business cards, carry them with you, and designate a time each day to review them.

PART THREE

EAT WITH SOMEONE

You were made to eat. But eating is about a lot more than fueling the body with flavors and foods. When God *blessed you to be a blessing,* He included eating as part of the blessing.

The average American consumes about one million calories a year, and in the best of worlds, burns about that many as well. These calories generate energy to keep the heart beating, the lungs breathing, the body warm, and to help you move through the world. The food itself is certainly a blessing. God has designed you to enjoy a remarkable variety of foods. From grass to grasshoppers, from cockroaches to cattle, from wax worms to wax beans, and on and on and on. We are fascinated with food. The Food Network goes 24/7 with instructions and competitions in the art of manipulating flavors. We live in an age of celebrity chefs who compete in kitchen stadiums.

The blessing is about more than food

But as I said, the blessing is about far more than the food. Historically speaking, the act of fueling the human body has always been a significantly social affair. Years ago, my mother-in-law went on a diet that consisted of a pill at meal time. Preparation involved pouring 10 ounces of water out of the tap and into a mug and drinking it with the pill. That was it. That was meal time. After a month or so, she made two observations. First, she had so much more time in her day since the preparation, consumption, and clean-up at meal time can take a lot of time. And secondly, she complained that she was lonely and bored.

"Interaction over food is the single most important feature of socializing," says Sidney Mintz, professor of anthropology at Johns Hopkins University. "The food becomes the carriage that conveys feelings back and forth."[1]

Cultures define themselves by the foods they eat. Most every life event is accompanied by a meal. Weddings, anniversaries, funerals, graduations, retirements, commencements, confirmations, celebrations—just about every social act comes with a meal attached.

As we've said, God made us to be social beings and the first not-good thing in the Bible is aloneness. The act of eating does more than fuel the body; it feeds us socially. My daughter, Traci, is a licensed counselor and social worker. For several years, she worked with troubled girls in public schools. As she described some of the sometimes funny and sometimes tragic choices they would make, I couldn't help asking whether she could see any common denominator. She said

1 *TIME* magazine, June 7, 2006.

it was nearly universally true that Dad was absent and Mom was uninvolved. As a result, they never ate meals together. They were left on their own to make up life for themselves.

Study after study underlines the impact that eating with others has on social, intellectual, emotional, and spiritual health.

Eating with others creates a sense of warmth and wellbeing, of belonging. It breaks down barriers to intimacy and feeds self-esteem. The family legacy of funny stories and significant moments are passed down.

Eating together models good manners and calls forth decency. It reduces the likelihood of bad habits and destructive behaviors. Many studies have shown that when families eat together, a sharp reduction occurs among children in terms of drug abuse and unhealthy sexual behaviors. Family meals help vaccinate against depression, suicide, eating disorders, and all sorts of destructive thinking.

We solve problems together while eating; we model the kinds of thinking and decision-making that help children understand critical thinking.

We make confessions while we eat and offer forgiveness. We repair and restore relationships.

Eating together expands our understanding of the world and other cultures and nourishes an appreciation for differing appetites.

Eating together teaches and refines language skills, not only technical, but also the emotional use of words and speech.

These studies also show that the significance and positive effect of the family meal grows even more important as our children age.

The human body's chemistry is finely tuned to tell us when we need food and also when we've had enough. But we should understand that the hunger for food is also the hunger for fellowship. The blessing of mealtime fellowship begins in the family's inner circle, but it radiates outward in concentric circles that include friends, neighbors, and workmates, and also includes strangers and even enemies.

Many significant events in the Bible are accompanied by a meal. The whole drama of God's activity in history is acted out in the Bible's two greatest meals—The Passover Meal and The Lord's Supper.

Jesus' last act with His disciples was a meal. This meal had such an impact that it's still celebrated today and remains one of God's chief resources for blessing people. After the resurrection, Jesus frequently appeared to His disciples while they were eating. When Jesus told His disciples to remember Him in eating the Bread and drinking the Cup, He was introducing them to the transformational power contained within a meal. Mealtimes come preloaded with sacramental potential. Jesus desires to come alive at mealtimes both to bless us and help us bless others.

Consider the Jesus-meal as the prototype for meals that bless. Meals that bless have certain characteristics. You don't have to be a priest or pastor to preside at a meal that blesses.

CHAPTER ONE

THE BLESSING:

Jesus Blesses with
Careful Preparation

The meal that blesses begins with preparation. In Jesus' day the Passover Meal required cleaning the house and assembling all the elements for a meal that included fifteen stages. Each stage was a kind of puzzle piece that, when fully assembled, told the story of God's love and His gift of deliverance from bondage. Jesus customized the Passover meal in a way that emphasized His own self-sacrificing and life-giving love.

Jesus told Peter and John to go into the city and find a man carrying a jar of water on his head who would take them to an upper room that was furnished for the meal. It's a small detail, but important because finding a room in Jerusalem during the Feast of Unleavened Bread would have been like finding a table at a restaurant on Mother's Day. If you don't make a reservation, you won't find a table.

Jesus blesses in advance

It's interesting that there was no place at the inn for Jesus in the first week of His life so He was born in a barn, and that

Jerusalem was so crowded on the last week of His life that He slept outside on the Mount of Olives. Jesus never had a place to lay His head. Jesus never owned anything—not a horse nor a house. But when it came to the last meal that He would share with His closest friends, He moved heaven and earth so He could personally make reservations in the overcrowded city of Jerusalem. The disciples noticed this action. It was an important detail to them, and so, alongside Jesus' profound teachings, His signs and wonders, His trial and crucifixion and resurrection, they also noted this otherwise obscure detail that when it came to His last meal on earth, Jesus made advance reservations and preparations.

Jesus blesses us by getting things ready in advance. There isn't a place you can go where He hasn't already been. There isn't an obstacle you confront that He hasn't found a way over, under, around, or through. There isn't a detail of your life that hasn't been investigated in advance.

When it was time for you to be born, you didn't make application, review potential family configurations, select calendar dates, skin color, or economic strata. No, you just opened your eyes and here you were, and you had nothing to do with any of it. Clearly, God had planned a life for you.

God's Word declares:

The One who has planned this whole experience for
you is God.
(1 Corinthians 5:5)

And according to the circumstances of God's design, you were not born into a hole in the ground, nor hanging from the limb of a tree, nor in an ooze of eggs on the underside of a lily pad. You were designed with the greatest care.

God's Word declares:

For it was you who formed my inward parts;
you knit me together in my mother's womb.

I praise you, for I am fearfully and wonderfully made.
Wonderful are your works;
that I know very well.
My frame was not hidden from you,
when I was being made in secret,
intricately woven in the depths of the earth.
Your eyes beheld my unformed substance.
In your book were written
all the days that were formed for me,
when none of them as yet existed.
(Psalm 139:13-16)

And when you were born, loving hands, which for months and years had awaited and planned and prepared for your arrival, were there to hold you and tend to your every need. Among all the creatures on planet earth, human beings possess the greatest potential and also require the longest and most intensive care before reaching that potential. We can't walk for a year, and we can't speak for two. At the very earliest, it's ten or fifteen years before we can fix our own food, find our own shelter, make our own living. From the beginning, we are dependent creatures who cannot survive unless someone prepares and provides for us.

God's Word declares:

> *For surely I know the plans I have for you, says the Lord,*
> *plans for your welfare and not for harm,*
> *to give you a future with hope.*
> (Jeremiah 29:12)

Abounding blessings await

And across the span of all your years, God has calculated your needs and prepared to sustain you. I read recently that the agricultural production potential of planet earth is sufficient to supply every human being with 2,500 calories of food a day. That's just about the perfect amount for healthy nutrition. God has clearly planned life for us on planet earth.

God's Word declares:

> *…the rain and the snow come down from heaven,*
> *and do not return there until they have watered the earth,*
> *making it bring forth and sprout,*

giving seed to the sower and bread to the eater.
(Isaiah 55:10)

We worry, we stew, we fret about the present and the future, but evidence is abundant and irrefutable that God has planned and prepared a life for us now...

And my God will fully satisfy every need of yours according to his riches in glory in Christ Jesus.
(Philippians 4:19)

...and forever:

I have told you that I go to prepare a place for you. And if I go and prepare a place for you, I will come again and will take you to myself, so that where I am, there you may be also.
(John 14:2)

God is the author of hospitality and His blessing begins with His elaborate and intentional preparations. We are, of course, not bound by this hospitality because God's *love does not insist on its own way.* That's why there is so much trouble and such crushing need in the world. Human beings habitually and willfully reject God's plan and distort His provision.

Yet even in the fallen, broken world, God continues, with the greatest creativity, to prepare and provide for us.

For while we were still weak, at the right time Christ died for the ungodly. Indeed, rarely will anyone die for a righteous person—though perhaps for a good person someone might actually

dare to die. But God proves his love for us in that while we still were sinners Christ died for us.
(Romans 5:6-8)

God is the chess-master. No move on the board can checkmate Him. When a huge and hungry crowd gathered around Jesus, He asked Philip:

'Where are we to buy bread for these people to eat?' He said this to test him, for He Himself knew what he was going to do.
(John 6:5-6)

Jesus always knows what He's going to do. He always has a plan. He is always prepared. From before you were born until this very moment, you haven't made a decision, or found yourself in a location where God has not already been preparing your way. From great to small, Jesus' preparations are part of His blessings—right down to the dinner table.

CHAPTER TWO

THE APPLICATION:
Bless Others with Careful Preparation

What we do in advance is an essential part of the way we
bless others. Many meals that God could have used to bless
others have never taken place because we haven't done the
advance planning.

Create a bless-list

It begins with the invitation list. An initial list of people
will usually easily come to mind—friends, neighbors, col-
leagues at work. Don't leave family off the list. For years
when our children were young, each week I'd stop at school
and pick one up to take to lunch. I got permission from the
principal and we followed the school's schedule. Now, even
decades later when our kids talk about important memories,
they mention when dad took them out of school and off
to lunch. And our children are never too old to invite to a
meal.

Make a list of people you'd like to bless by thanking them
for their influence in your life. They may have no idea that

a word they said or work they have done has made a difference in your life.

Be on the lookout for people you'd like to get to know and people you'd like to introduce to others. Add people who seem lost and lonely, keeping in mind that the Bible says:

Do not neglect to show hospitality to strangers, for by doing that some have entertained angels without knowing it.
(Hebrews 13:2)

Jesus went out of His way to eat with people who were broken, lost and lonely. Remember Zacchaeus? (Luke 19:1-10)

And include the people with whom you need to repair relationships. Remember the old axiom: "Stay close to your friends—and closer to your enemies." Life moves at the speed of friendship, so sharing a meal, even with an enemy, has the power to transform a relationship. Psalm 23 offers the intriguing observation: *You prepare a table before me in the presence of my enemies.* It could be that God will use a meal to repair a broken relationship. The Bible says:

If your enemies are hungry, give them something to eat. If they are thirsty, give them something to drink…
(Romans 12:20)

Make your calendar a tool for blessing

Get it on your calendar. Many of the most important meals of our lives have not yet taken place simply because we haven't put them on the calendar. Some of our best work has never been done because of the calendar. Some of our greatest opportunities have never materialized because of our calendar. Some of the best friends we've never had are because of the calendar. The saddest words in any language surely must be the words, *too late*. The calendar is, of course, a difficult and many-headed monster to manage. Few things have the power to produce regret like an unmanaged calendar.

Let the blessing consume you

And finally, when you've made the invitation and finished the arrangements—relax! An uptight meal is no blessing. I remember what may have been the first dinner invitation Terri and I received after entering the ministry. A sweet woman in the church invited the "new young pastor and his wife" to dinner. We could tell from the start that our hostess was wound one turn too tight. After a few minutes in the living room, we were brought to the dining room and assigned our seats. The conversation was formal. We sat up straight, not even daring to lean back because that seemed too casual. We put napkins in laps and offered a prayer. The table had been extended to accommodate the guests and our hostess was seated over one of the extensions. She picked up her fork to signal that eating was permitted, and just as she did, the table extension collapsed, spilling the entire plate of lasagna into her lap. She gasped. All the oxygen left the room. Time froze. After a pause, she gathered up her plate into her skirt and waddled out of the room. No one moved. Not a word was spoken. Not a breath was taken. History stopped for five minutes until she reappeared, wearing an entirely different outfit. And it was like someone touched the "play" key and the dinner resumed as if nothing had ever happened. And she never said a word about it.

Relaxation is also part of the preparation, and it's an essential part of the blessing.

Recently, I got curious about the need to double-click the mouse on my computer. Wikipedia explains that the first click helps you to select an action and the second click allows you to execute the action. When it comes to many of the most important transactions of life, we live between the "clicks." With relative ease, we make the selection, but we often fail when it comes to execution. Life moves at the speed of the second click. Jesus lived before computers, but He knew all about the importance of the double click. To pass God's blessings along to others at mealtime requires that you first "select," and second, that you "execute."

DIALOGUE BOX

Your journal

In what ways does the experience of eating impact your day?

Your prayers

Make a list of the kinds of food you enjoy most and thank God for them.

Your discussion

- Describe some of the favorite meals you can remember and what you enjoyed about them.

- What elements of hospitality and preparation are most/least natural to you?

Your memory

Isaiah 55:2

Your action

- Develop a list of occasions you could celebrate over a meal.

- Identify three meals you'd like to host, set the date, and make the invitation—get it on the calendar.

CHAPTER THREE

THE BLESSING:
Jesus' Heart is Turned Toward You

As important as it is to set the table, it's even more important to prepare the heart. Jesus said:

> *I have eagerly desired to share this meal with you before*
> *I suffer.*
> (Luke 22:15)

Raising blessings above circumstance

Eagerly desired? Really? Think of His circumstance. Jesus was stepping into the lowest moment in the history of the world. In an hour, Judas would betray Him. Meanwhile, His disciples were busy bickering over popularity and position, and Peter had separated himself from everyone in a spirit of smug superiority. These were not their best moments. The world was at its worst and so were Jesus' best friends. Who could have blamed Jesus for wringing His hands and whining, "Ain't it awful?" And yet, Jesus rose to the occasion—no, He rose *above* the occasion and declared, "I have eagerly desired to share this meal with you." And if

He hadn't? If instead He had sulked or pouted or scolded or stomped away, do you really think that after 2,000 years, the world would still approach the Lord's Supper with such frequency and reverence?

The only reason this meal turned out to be a blessing was because Jesus turned the angle of His heart to catch a ray of light to shine into the darkness of that dinner gathering.

Some people say that the most famous story Jesus ever told was the Parable of the Prodigal Son (Luke 15). The story tells us a lot about the angle of Jesus' heart. It's the story of a boy who used his father's money to get as far away from his father as he possibly could—in every way—physically, socially, emotionally, morally, and spiritually. Ultimately, the young man became a slave in a foreign land where he was starving. With a mouth full of humble pie, he decided to return and to ask his father to hire him as a slave. The big surprise came when it turned out to be the father who ran to greet and embrace the son. The New Revised Version of the Bible translates this, "while he was still far off," suggesting that he still hadn't quite escaped the far country. What a hope-filled idea. The father's heart had always been turned toward the son, ever since the moment the boy turned and walked away—even when he was still in the far country.

Every parent feels a kinship with the father in Jesus' story. I imagine the father rearranging the household furniture so that everywhere he went in the house, he could see deep into the far country to catch a glimpse of his son coming home. Even when the son's heart was turned away from the father, the father's heart remained steadfastly turned toward the son.

I saw a mom in the mall the other day. She had three young children. The youngest she carried in a kind of sling held over her shoulder, the next she pushed in a stroller, and the oldest she let walk a little ahead on a leash. The older the child, the longer the leash. That's the way parenting works; it's the process of releasing our children by inches until we let go of the leash altogether. For me, gradually releasing children was an anxious process. When our children started driving, I could never go to sleep until the last child was home. I couldn't count the number of hours I've spent well past midnight staring out the bay window, straining my eyes to the end of the street, hoping to catch the first glimmer of a headlight signaling their safe return. My heart has always been turned toward my children.

Jesus didn't just tell the story of the Prodigal Son as a philosophical exercise; the story was a description of the way Jesus lived His life. And it was about more than family—it was about all of humanity. It was the angle of Jesus' heart toward humanity, in all its sinful brokenness, that saved the world. And the angle of Jesus' heart was always turned toward the disciples. For this reason, He could say, even when they were in the far country of their betrayal and bickering,

I have eagerly desired to share this meal with you before I suffer.
If this desire had not been true, everything about that meal
would have been different. If Jesus' heart had been as hard
as His disciples' hearts, if He had allowed a spirit of smug
superiority to settle in, if He had descended into pettiness,
if He had been plotting ways to get even, this meal would
not have become a sacramental bridge connecting heaven
and earth.

Blessing the imperfect

A meal doesn't have to be perfect to be a blessing. If the
Lord's Supper is a kind of prototype meal for blessing others, it's important to notice how much time is given to describing all the trouble Jesus and the disciples were having
at the table. It's tempting to romanticize the Last Supper,
but in reality, it was like many of our meals. It was enough
to test even Jesus' goodwill. During this meal, Jesus was surprisingly candid about such troubles. And Jesus confronted
each with creative grace. Even a messed up meal can produce blessings.

At this meal, Jesus didn't just turn His heart toward the disciples; He also reached out to them physically. He broke
the bread and gave it to them. He poured out the cup and
handed it to them. He knelt down and washed their feet.
These were more than acts of simple courtesy and hospitality. They were Jesus' way of stepping in His disciples' direction and into their world.

Judas was struggling with temptation. We are told that the devil had put it into Judas' heart to betray Jesus. Think of it. Jesus shared this meal with a man who was considering ways to destroy Him. Certainly, betrayal is the deepest form of hostility of which human beings are capable. During supper, Judas was mulling it over in his mind. Should he or shouldn't he betray Jesus? Can anything be more disheartening than to know that the person across from you is plotting to destroy you or some facet of your life? To steal your spouse. To destroy your reputation. To turn people against you with lies. To take your business. To undermine your well-being. To assault your convictions. To sow seeds of anxiety and inferiority.

Would you put a man like Judas on your invitation list? Why would you invite someone to eat with you who was planning to betray you? It's possible that Jesus was reaching out to Judas one more time. Jesus knew Judas was the betrayer, but He gave him the bread and cup anyway—His body broken and His blood poured out—one last time, Jesus gave Himself away to Judas. Remember, *Love never ends* (1 Corinthians 13:8).

The disciples had wandered into the wilderness of comparisons. Each of them wanted to be somebody. I can sympathize. I have an ugly, anxious little man living inside of me who spends a lot of time shouting at the top of his lungs, "See, I really am somebody!" But all of our efforts to get ahead, to make a name for ourselves, to be somebody, come at the expense of others.

For his part, Peter had determined he was better than the others.

Peter said to him, 'Though all become deserters because of you, I will never desert you.'
(Matthew 26:33)

Blessings make things beautiful

Each disciple in his own way was leaning out of the circle. It was only Jesus who leaned in. It was only Jesus who reached out. At the table, Jesus did everything He could to tip the disciples in a different direction, a better direction. His efforts call to mind for me Cesar Millan, who hosts a television show called *The Dog Whisperer*. Cesar has a gift for working with difficult dogs. Even a simple thing like taking a dog for a walk can turn into a nightmare. Some dogs turn to stone when put on a leash. Some dogs strain and gag at the end of a leash. Cesar Millan uses a kind of pull and release method. First, he puts the leash high on the dog's neck to pull its nose out of the dirt; then, he applies a series of pull-and-release actions. His point is not to force the dog forward but to lift the dog's head and coax the dog to a better place. Jesus seemed to apply a similar approach to His disciples. He reached out to them, and with acts of *compassion, kindness,*

humility, meekness, patience, forbearance, forgiveness, and love,
He tried to rock them in a better direction.

Perhaps the most intense explosion of light in that meal
came when Jesus reached out to His disciples to wash their
feet. At the table, the disciples had been struggling with
comparisons. There's some suggestion that the trouble started when the disciples looked around the table and noticed
the seating arrangements and who was sitting where. When
is it that we become aware of our "place" in the world? Is it
in nursery school? Is it before that? Who's first and who's
last? Who's best and worst? Most popular and least popular?

Jesus' first reaction was to remind the disciples that His followers needed to work out of a different operating system.
Then Jesus took off His outer robe, tied a towel around His
waist, took a basin, and began washing the disciples' feet.
He blessed them with His humility. What Jesus did was so
unexpected that Peter complained about it:

> *Lord, are you going to wash my feet...*
> *You will never wash my feet.*
> (John 13:6-8)

When Jesus finished washing their feet, He put His robe
back on and said:

> *You call me teacher and Lord—and you are right, for that is*
> *what I am. So if I, your Lord and teacher, have washed your*
> *feet, you also should wash one another's feet...if you know*

these things, how blessed are you if you do them.
(John 13:13-17)

It is overwhelming to be confronted by true humility. The truly humble person is profoundly beautiful. The truly humble person is influential out of all proportion to expectation. The act of true humility is perhaps the most intensely beautiful act of which humans are capable. Humility is the substance of every other fruit of the spirit.

The *Diagnostic and Statistical Manual of Mental Disorders* includes something called "The Stendhal Syndrome," named after the nineteenth century French writer who was overcome while visiting Santa Croche, the extraordinary multi-hued marble cathedral in Florence, Italy. More than 100 other tourists have also been overwhelmed while visiting there. Symptoms include heart palpitations and light-headedness that sometimes even require hospitalization. The cause, they have determined, is not something in the water or the air, but the sheer beauty of the place. The Stendhal Syndrome refers to the phenomena of being overwhelmed by beauty. Jesus' beautiful act of humility at the table that day was overwhelming to the disciples and it has become the standard for behavior since then.

If the environment at mealtime decays, and animosities and anxieties begin to show, it's still possible for the meal to offer a blessing if someone at the table can follow Jesus' example of humility and service. And it will be beautiful.

To give yourself away—broken and poured out—to empty yourself has the power to move people to a better place. That's what Jesus did at the table—He did something bigger than Judas' betrayal and the disciples' arguing.

This is My Body... This is My Blood...

Jesus reached out with something bigger and more beautiful to rock them in the direction of a blessing. This meal became a blessing because of the angle of Jesus' heart and the reach of His hand.

CHAPTER FOUR

THE APPLICATION:
Turn Your Heart Toward Others

There's nothing quite like being around good-willed and cheerful people. Who really wants to be around a sourpuss? Who wants to be around a whiner? Who wants to be around a critic? And mealtime grumpiness is worse than rubber chicken. If you want to bless others by eating with them, then begin by being in a good mood. Begin by turning your heart toward others.

This statement is easier said than done. People are difficult, and being a decent person is difficult, too. And you never know what might come up during a meal. The wrong look or the wrong word can ignite a firestorm, and you never know when it might occur. So be prepared.

Reflecting blessings

Before plunging into a meal, remember what you have been told about blessing others so when the unexpected erupts at the meal, you'll be prepared to keep the blessings moving despite the unforeseen obstacles.

Guard your heart with all vigilance for from it flow the
springs of life.
(Proverbs 4:23)

The ancient Egyptians illuminated the pyramids' pitch-black inner chambers by positioning and angling polished mirrors to catch and reflect the light of the sun. With the mirrors, they made light bend, rise, and descend. Jesus set the angle of His life to reflect light into every situation. Like Jesus, we bless people by setting the angle of our heart to catch His light and reflect it into our corner of life. Remember that all goodness is reflected goodness. It all originates from God.

Every generous act of giving, with every perfect gift, is from
above, coming down from the Father of lights, with whom
there is no variation or shadow due to change.
(James 1:17)

So position yourself in such a way that allows Jesus' light to pour onto you and through you. Jesus was once criticized for showing great kindness and mercy to a sin-plagued woman. She was so astonished and grateful that she knelt at Jesus' feet and wept. His critics growled, "Doesn't He know what kind of woman this is?" To them, Jesus said:

I tell you, her sins, which were many, have been forgiven;
hence she has shown great love. But the one to whom little is
forgiven, loves little.'
(Luke 7:47)

Jesus was shining a beam of light into that dinner conversation. Jesus forgives us excessively so that we can forgive others excessively.

When the Bible describes the fruit of the Spirit, it's really a listing of beams of light designed to be reflected from God through us to others.

The fruit of the Spirit is love, joy, peace, patience, kindness, generosity, faithfulness, gentleness, and self-control. There is no law against such things. And those who belong to Christ Jesus have crucified the flesh with its passions and desires. If we live by the Spirit, let us also be guided by the Spirit.
(Galatians 5:22-25)

When you sit at a table with others and the mood becomes unloving, adjust the angle of your life to catch the *love of God* and reflect it into that moment.

When at the table the conversation grows gloomy, whiney, and sour, adjust the angle of your life to catch the *joy of God* and reflect it into that moment.

When the table conversation slips toward tension and hostility, adjust the angle of your life to catch the *peace of God* and reflect it into the moment.

When the mood at the table becomes anxious and aggressive, adjust the angle of your life to reflect the *patience of God* into the moment.

When the conversation at the table trends toward what's critical and judgmental, adjust the angle of your life to reflect the *kindness of God* into the moment.

When the environment at the table turns petty and selfish, adjust the angle of your life to reflect the *generosity of God* into the moment.

When the environment at the table becomes incompatible with the purposes of God, adjust the angle of your life to reflect the *faithfulness of God* into the moment.

When the temperature at the table turns hostile and corrosive, adjust the angle of your life to reflect the *gentleness of God* into the moment.

When the tone at the table descends into vulgarity and ugliness, adjust the angle of your life to reflect the *self-control of God* into the movement.

Make your blessings bigger than anything that blows up at the table

Don't be surprised to find people leaning into the darkness at the table. For Judas, it was the darkness of spiritual warfare and temptation. For the other disciples, it was the dark cloud of comparisons. We have a deep yearning to "be somebody." Our hunger for this recognition can be insatiable. Some interesting research has been done on Olympic medalists that suggests the bronze and gold medalists are the happiest medalists, while the silver medal is the saddest. Apparently, if you win the bronze you are happy because if you hadn't won it, you wouldn't have won anything. And if you win the gold, you are happy because that means you're the best in the world. But if you win the silver medal, you are plagued with sadness over what might have been. People have an acute sensitivity over their place in the world.

Michaele and Tareq Salahi made international headlines when they somehow managed to get through several checkpoints and security screenings to join a White House reception that President Obama was hosting for Indian Prime Minister Manmohan Singh. Within two hours of the event, Mrs. Salahi was posting photos of herself with President Obama and Vice President Biden and a host of celebrities who had been officially invited to the gathering. And also within hours, the United States Secret Service, Department of Homeland Security, and United States Congress had launched investigations and were considering possible criminal charges. What was the Salahis' offense? It was simple. They were socially out-of-place. They had not been invited.

A certain man in Houston faked his Vietnam War record. He bought medals and battle ribbons in thrift stores and sewed them on his uniform. He created accounts of courage and heroism. He told and retold the stories so often that he began to believe them himself. The Buffalo Soldiers National Museum in Houston even created a display of his war record. His story was told on the evening news. But then someone got curious and did the research and discovered it was all a fabrication. When the truth came out, the man tried to explain that his whole life he'd been a nobody and he just wanted to be somebody.

The Jesus-life is not like what you might expect. It is not a quest for medals or notoriety. It's not designed to make you rich or famous or powerful or influential—it's designed to make you humble. It is designed to make you somebody in a completely different way than you would expect. Jesus asked the disciples:

> *Who is greater, the one who is at the table or the one who serves? Is it not the one at the table?*

That's the operating system with which the disciples were familiar. But then Jesus went on to turn life upside down by saying:

> *But I am among you as one who serves. He told them, the greatest among you must become like the youngest and the leader like one who serves.*
> (Luke 22:26-27)

I once heard Bill Hybels, pastor of Willowcreek Church, describe this as "downward mobility." It's life powered by humility from knee-level. The Bible puts it this way:

Do nothing from selfish ambition or conceit, but in humility
regard others as better than yourself…look not after your own
interests, but to the interests of others. Let the same mind be in
you that was in Christ Jesus.

(Philippians 2:3-5)

When Hannah Teter won the gold medal in the 2006
Olympic Halfpipe competition, she got rich and famous.
It could have gone to her head. But as a little girl, Hannah
always had a vision of herself as a helpful person. So she gave
away all her winnings to supply clean water to the children
who live in an orphanage in the Kirindon Community in
Kenya. She considers herself blessed to be a blessing. The
need to be somebody can ruin a meal. The quest for position
and place can extinguish a blessing. It's tempting when you
sit at the table to go on about "your medals." But blessings
do not move when egos are involved. Egos shrink blessings
to nothing. Humility is what's needed. Blessings move on
the shoulders of humble people. Humility is a ray of light.

Currently, the world's largest solar power plant can be found
in eastern Portugal. It looks like a massive field of mechani-
cal sunflowers. The plant consists of 2,520 gleaming, polished house-sized solar panels that are technically as sophisticated as your automobile. Each panel is carefully shaped
to catch the rays of the sun and reflect them toward a tower
where their heat is captured and transformed into power.
The most interesting feature is the way each panel tilts at a

perfect angle to the sun and follows the movement of the sun as it sweeps every day across the sky through 240 degrees of its great arc.

The population of the world just passed 7 billion. It's estimated that 2.1 billion of that total are Christians. Imagine the impact on history if each of us were diligently committed to positioning the angle of our lives every day to catch the light of God and reflect it into the moment where we lived?

At dinner a very long time ago, Jesus turned His heart to reflect the fullness of God's light into the darkest moment in history. The moment was so powerful and so profound that His followers have never stopped talking about and never stopped replaying the moment ever since. A meal is the perfect place to reflect light into darkness and bless the people who are there. But it only turned out this way because Jesus did something bigger.

Rob Bell tells of going to Rwanda. He was met by a woman named Phyllis. She said, "Come see my dying friend." They threaded their way through the muddy alleys of the slums until they found the room. The man had only hours to live. He was covered with filth and disease. Phyllis knelt down and took him in her arms and wept. But her weeping did something to the room. Her weeping seemed to conquer the agony of disease, the stench of death, the oppressive darkness. Her compassionate weeping was bigger than all these things. Her weeping brought light into the darkness. Blessing others requires doing something bigger—more compassionate, more loving, more gracious, more forgiving, more creative. These "bigger" blessings eclipse the size of the misery.[1]

If the environment at mealtime decays, and animosities and anxieties begin to show, it's still possible for the meal to offer a blessing if someone at the table can follow Jesus' example of humility and service and do something bigger than the decay, animosity, and anxiety. And it can be the most beautiful meal in the world.

---

1 Rob Bell, *Velvet Elvis*, 74.

DIALOGUE BOX

Your journal

Write about the current condition of your heart and how it impacts your daily life.

Your prayers

Lift up before God the areas of your life that are in need of Divine healing.

Your discussion

- Describe some mental disciplines that would assist God in the transformation of your heart.

- Discuss some of the things you can do that might "tip" people in the direction of reconciliation.

Your memory

Proverbs 4:23

Your action

- In light of these things, make a list of three things you need to remind yourself about in an uncomfortable social situation.

- Identify a broken relationship in your life and apply to it one of the actions listed in the discussion section above.

CHAPTER FIVE

THE BLESSING:

Jesus Prays for You

While Judas was planning his betrayal and the disciples were jockeying for position and power, Simon Peter was feeling smug and superior. By all gospel accounts, Jesus had special leadership responsibilities in mind for Peter, but as yet, Peter didn't understand what that leadership meant. It appears that Peter thought it meant he would not be susceptible to the weaknesses that would afflict the other disciples. He famously pronounced, *Even if all these others abandon You, I won't. I'll even die with You.* Of all the things Peter wished he'd never said, those words may top the list.

It is a painful truth in life that we are always just a heartbeat away from being the worst person we can imagine being. I was driving on the freeway one day behind a trailer full of gravel. The pile of gravel had no cover and sharp little stones were spraying out like missiles. I could hear them pinging against my hood and windshield, so I couldn't wait to get away from the trailer. People can be like that too—like a loose load of gravel nicking and wounding others with little words and attitudes that leave them bloodied and scarred. You want to get away from people like that. That's how Satan divides people. He likes to make a big deal out of our little flaws. If you want to bless others, be sure to check to see what's blowing off the trailer behind you. Any little character flaw or comment can make a big mess of a meal. If you want your meal to bless, be on guard for these things and be prepared with the countermeasures of grace and kindness.

So here was Simon Peter, sitting at the table, overly self-assured that he possessed strengths of character that the other disciples lacked. How do you add a blessing to a person who's already full of himself? Everyone agrees that it's no fun being with arrogant people. But Jesus knew the truth about Simon. He knew the character flaws that were gnawing away at Peter's inner world. So Jesus offered two instructions to Simon Peter that we would all do well to remember, especially at mealtime.

First, Jesus warned Simon Peter:

> *Satan has demanded to sift all of you like wheat.*
> (Luke 22:31)

The diamond is the hardest substance on earth, but if you know where to strike it, you can shatter it in pieces. Jesus knew Satan very well and understood that little flaws were Satan's playground. Evil has perfected the art of appearing insignificant. The biggest dangers we face in life often come in the smallest packages. So when you pull yourself up to the table with a plan to pass on a blessing, watch out for little things. Jesus said:

> *...whoever is faithful in very little is faithful also in much, and whoever is dishonest in very little is dishonest also in much.*
>
> (Luke 16:10)

Peter's private little attitude of smug superiority had the power to split the atom and separate him from the disciples. Jesus warned Simon that the greatest threat to the disciples would not come from the outside world of clubs and swords, but from their private individual inner world of attitudes and ambitions.

The stunningly simple blessings

It's not usually the big things that fragment the human community. Most people manage to avoid the major sins. Instead, it's the little things. So Jesus warned Peter:

> *Satan has demanded to sift all of you like wheat.*
>
> (Luke 22:31)

Satan intends to divide us up and separate us from each other like wheat that is divided and sifted. But after this warning, Jesus went on to promise Peter:

> *I have prayed for you....*
>
> *(Luke 22:32)*

And it's so stunningly simple.

I have prayed for you that your own faith may not fail; and
you, once you have turned back, strengthen your brothers.
(Luke 22:32)

Prayer was Jesus' antidote for the dark power of the devil and for the deep vulnerability of our blind overconfidence. Prayer is the centerpiece of all blessings.

So much was going on at that table; so many potential road-blocks existed to blessing. And perhaps prayer doesn't sound like much. Don't we need something more substantial than a prayer? As Dale Bruner once said, "Don't we need therapy, a 12-Step Program, coaching, cheerleading, decisive divine intervention?" But Jesus says, *I have prayed for you!*

Ironically, in just a few hours, Peter would spit out a curse on Jesus and swear that he never even knew his friend. He'd find himself alone and weeping bitterly. That's the way it is in the circle of human life. Everyone knows what it's like to be Humpty Dumpty and to take a great fall. Conventional wisdom says that fallen people can't be put back together again. As usual, Jesus breaks with such pessimist conclusions. Jesus' main plan for putting Peter's life back together was to pray for him.

Jesus sees the whole spectrum of blessings flowing on the currents of prayer. And Jesus demonstrated a profound simplicity and intensity to prayer. When His disciples asked for His teaching on prayer, He replied simply:

> *Our Father in heaven,*
> *hallowed be your name.*
>
> *Your kingdom come.*
> *Your will be done,*
> *on earth as it is in heaven.*
> *Give us this day our daily bread.*
> *And forgive us our debts,*
> *as we also have forgiven our debtors.*
> *And do not bring us to the time of trial,*
> *but rescue us from the evil one.*
> (Matthew 6:9-13)

Jesus came to the tomb of Lazarus. He was preparing to call forth the dead! And this was His prayer:

> *Father, I thank you for having heard me. I knew that you always hear me, but I have said this for the sake of the crowd standing here, so that they may believe that you sent me.*
> (John11:41-42)

So simple.

He taught His disciples:

> *But whenever you pray, go into your room and shut the door and pray to your Father who is in secret; and your Father who sees in secret will reward you. When you are praying, do not*

heap up empty phrases as the Gentiles do; for they think that
they will be heard because of their many words.

(Matthew 6:6-7)

Jesus' own prayer life appeared to be both simple and continuous. It was not so much an activity as it was a way of living continuously and openly before God – not an occasional activity, but an all-consuming lifestyle.

I struggle with prayer as a formal activity. I am embarrassed by how short my attention span is for formal prayer. But strangely, when my prayer life becomes a running dialogue— a continuous, unbroken conversation with the Living God, it's easier. This prayer life does not always succeed in finding words. But it doesn't matter. St. Paul assured us:

Likewise the Spirit helps us in our weakness; for we do not
know how to pray as we ought, but that very Spirit intercedes
with sighs too deep for words. And God, who searches the
heart, knows what is the mind of the Spirit, because the Spirit
intercedes for the saints according to the will of God.

(Romans 8:26-27)

I remember hearing of a pastor who was called to a woman's bedside in the last hours of her life. The woman was plagued by a deep guilt over what she considered to have been a wasted life and a string of broken relationships both in her family and with God. She knew how disappointed God must be with her. The pastor noticed a photo of a young woman on the dresser. When he asked about the photo, the woman answered that it was her daughter, and that even though she hadn't seen her in years, she always kept the photo in a place where she could see it. And the pastor paused and said, "God has a photo of you on His dresser."

If Jesus has a dresser, He has a photo of you on it. You are ever before Him and He sees you and prays for you. These were very nearly Jesus' last words to Simon Peter.

I have prayed for you that your own faith may not fail; and you, once you have turned back, strengthen your brothers.
(Luke 22:32)

He spoke these words at dinner, and they became for Peter, a blessing.

CHAPTER SIX

THE APPLICATION:
Pray for Others

Jesus taught about prayer in a way that emphasized its simplicity. Not its length. Not its vocabulary. Not our posture or location. My friend Dale Bruner makes the outline for prayer easy to remember. He says, "Follow the BIF formula. Make your prayers *Brief, Intense,* and *Frequent.*"

Prayer is the constant reorientation of one's whole life toward God. It is the putting of one's whole life "in a different light"—in the Light of Christ. And in that light you see yourself, your circumstances, and others entirely differently.

My friend, Richard Lindermanis, battled cancer for years. He endured every known treatment and several major surgeries. Awakening after one surgery, he lay flat on his hospital mattress and said, rather groggily, "When I awoke from the anesthesia, I had the sense that I was lying on the most comfortable mattress I'd ever experienced. I looked over the edge of the bed and realized it wasn't a mattress at all. It was hands—hundreds and hundreds of hands. And I realized these were the hands of the people who were holding me up in prayer."

Prayer for others—your greatest form of blessing

The greatest blessing you can offer people is to pray for them—to hold them up before God. It's the most important element of being blessed and blessing others, and it's the element most easily neglected.

Louis Oosthuizen was the surprise winner of the 2010 British Open—by seven strokes. He built an early lead and everyone waited for his collapse. But it never came. On the thumb of his golf glove, Oosthuizen had marked a large red dot with his pen. When asked about it by a television reporter, he explained, "When the pressure intensified and my mind was exploding with 1,000 thoughts, I reminded myself to concentrate on the red dot. It centered me."

Mark a red dot somewhere in your life to remind yourself to pray. Satan has no countermeasure for it.

Keep a prayer list with people's names. Don't worry about words; just hold people up before God. Let them know you are praying—that's part of the blessing.

Because of a strange twist in God's gracious goodness, Terri and I have become acquainted with President George and Mrs. Barbara Bush. After my first brain surgery a few years back, Mrs. Bush came hustling across a room full of people to hug me and say, "I'm so glad to see you. I was praying for you just this morning." I was stunned at the idea that Barbara Bush remembered me and prayed for me. At that moment, Barbara Bush passed the blessing God gave to Abraham right along through history to me.

Marilynne Robinson's Pulitzer Prize winning novel, *Gilead*, includes a conversation between a Presbyterian pastor and his best friend's son—a young man who had always been the apple of his father's eye—and a continuous disappointment. It had come to a place where they could no longer even speak. Although the father was dying, the son determined that it was best that he leave town. The old pastor resented the boy for abandoning his father on his death bed, but even so, he felt strangely moved by God to bless the young man as he left town. After giving him twenty dollars, he said:

> "The thing I would like, actually, is to bless you." And in light of all the betrayals and disappointments that desire came as a complete surprise. The young man asked, "What would that involve?"

> "Well, as I envisage it, it would involve my placing my hand on your brow and asking the protection of God for you. But if it would be embarrassing"—There were a few people on the street.

> "No, no," he said. "That doesn't matter." And he took his hat off and set it on his knee and closed his eyes

and lowered his head, almost rested it against my hand, and I did bless him to the limit of my powers, whatever they are, repeating the benediction from Numbers, of course—"The Lord bless thee and keep thee; the Lord make His face to shine upon thee and be gracious unto thee: the Lord lift up His countenance upon thee, and give thee peace." Nothing could be more beautiful than that, or more expressive of my feelings, certainly, or more sufficient, for that matter. Then when he didn't open his eyes or lift his head, I said, "Lord, bless John Ames Boughton, this beloved son and brother and husband and father." Then he sat back and looked at me as if he were waking out of a dream.

"Thank you, Reverend," he said, and his tone made me think that to him it might have seemed I had just named everything I thought he no longer was, when that was absolutely the furthest thing from my meaning, the exact opposite of my meaning. Well, anyway, I told him it was an honor to bless him. And that was also absolutely true. In fact I'd have gone through seminary and ordination and all the years intervening for that one moment.[1]

To receive and to give blessings is the whole point of life. This act gives meaning to everything else that we do. Before there was a Bible, before there were commandments, before

---

1 Marilynne Robinson. *Gilead*, 241-2.

there was a temple for worship or priests, or prophets, there
was God's word to Abraham:

> *I will bless you...and in you I will bless all the families
> of the earth.*
> (Genesis 12:2-3)

All that God does and all that God intends to do through
us can be traced back to the act of blessing others. Not just
the good people or the faithful people or the compassionate
people or the generous people—ALL the people. It's easy to
wonder why you should bless others if they don't deserve it.
But it appears that if there's to be hope for the world, that
hope comes as God's people bless other people. The Bible
says:

> *Do you not know that it is the kindness of the Lord that is
> meant to turn your life around?*
> (Romans 2:4)

Kindness carries transformational power.

The greatest meal in history was full of high drama and many
obstacles to blessing, but Jesus demonstrated the power of
blessings in a meal. The BLESS Challenge invites you to *Eat
with Someone*. And it's about more than fueling the body. It's
about passing on a blessing and pronouncing a benediction
on that person's life.

DIALOGUE BOX

Your journal

In what ways does prayer impact your life?

Your prayers

Pray the Lord's Prayer (Matthew 6:9-13), meditating on each phrase.

Your discussion

- If you really believed these phrases to be true, how would it change your behavior?

- When does prayer seem most authentic and alive to you?

Your memory

Romans 2:4

Your action

- Read Romans 8:26-27 and use it as a guide for your prayer.

- Take the newspaper or go online to a news outlet and pray for the stories that make up the news.

PART FOUR

STUDY JESUS

You were made to study Jesus. After all, He's the model human being and the most important person who ever lived. A number of years ago, the Grosset and Dunlap Publishing House commissioned twenty-eight educators and historians to determine the most important events in history. Tops on their list was the discovery of America. Second was Gutenberg's invention of the moveable type printing press. Eleven things tied for third. In fourth place were the writing of the U.S. Constitution, the development of ether and the X-ray, human flight, and the life of Jesus. But of course, Jesus is not tied with anyone for fourth place. He's not even alone in fourth place. Jesus is preeminent in history. He is the Name above all names. He is the origin of history, the subject of history, and the destiny of history.

In their book *What If Jesus Had Never Been Born?*, D. James Kennedy and Jerry Newcombe reviewed Jesus' impact on history and concluded that in virtually every aspect of human life, Jesus' influence has been profound. Take Jesus out of history and the arts, social and physical sciences, education, health care, government, finance, and civilization itself would be profoundly impacted, rendered perhaps even unrecognizable in its present forms. As James Allen Francis famously wrote in 1926 in "One Solitary Life":

> *Jesus is the central figure of the human race*
> *And the leader of mankind's progress*
> *All the armies that have ever marched*
> *All the navies that have ever sailed*
> *All the parliaments that have ever sat*
> *All the kings that ever reigned put together*
> *Have not affected the life of mankind on earth*
> *As powerfully as that one solitary life.*

In Genesis 12, God restarted history. God told Abraham:

> *I will bless you, and make your name great, so that you will be*
> *a blessing. I will bless those who bless you...and in you all the*
> *families of the earth shall be blessed.*
> *(Genesis 12:2)*

Jesus is the fulfillment of God's plan to bless the families of the world. To prove it, Matthew reconstructed Jesus' family tree and traced it back to Abraham. Jesus is God's original blessing!

A blessed view of you

We study Jesus not just because of His astonishing attributes but because He is the model human being. He is the prototype of what we are designed to be. He is *the new Adam,* meaning that He is the original version of what God had in mind for us before the Fall.

If you want to know where you came from and where you are going, study Jesus. If you want to know the kind of person you are supposed to be and the way you are supposed to live, study Jesus. The miraculous and mysterious thing about studying Jesus is that, in doing so, you discover yourself. Jesus is the most direct route to the truest form of you!

When I moved to Houston a number of years ago, I found myself in a flat world with no familiar reference points. I was perpetually lost until I discovered the secret of Westheimer Road. In Houston, Westheimer Road extends from downtown to the far western suburbs. I figured out that from anywhere in the city, if I could find my way to Westheimer, I could find my way home. Find your way to Jesus and you'll find your way to your truest self.

Jesus is so dynamic that He contains within Himself all the infinite variety of personality types and individual qualities of all the people who have lived, are living, or ever will live. Contained within Jesus is the perfected version of every person who has ever or will ever exist. Contained within Jesus is the perfect version of the person who is uniquely you.

It's quite amazing that as humanity imitates Jesus, He doesn't make everyone alike, He makes everyone uniquely different—but different in ways that are mutually complementary. No greater blessing exists than studying Jesus. And the more you study Jesus and become like Him, the more you become a blessing to others.

Vows that break blessings

But here's the question: If Jesus is history's most powerful and influential person, and if living His kind of life makes us fully at home within ourselves, then why are we so reluctant to imitate Him? Why are we so willfully and habitually disobedient? Why do we so consistently second-guess His instructions? Why do we so often think that we have a better idea? If Jesus is the true-north of life, why do we all end up lost in the southern hemisphere so far from our intended design and destiny?

In the Disney movie *The Kid,* Russ Duritz is an image consultant, but he's also self-absorbed and insensitive. By the measure of wealth, he is a success. By the measure of humanity, he's a flop. A few days before his fortieth birthday, Russ meets a boy named Rusty, who, it turns out, is himself—but thirty-two years younger as an almost eight-year-old boy. Russ gets to see what he was like as a boy, and Rusty gets to see what he will be like as a man. Rusty discovers that the great plans he had for himself as a boy have not come true. Instead, he has emotional and relational problems, and he lives alone without a wife, a child, or even a dog. Finally, Rusty explodes, "How did I grow up to be a dogless, chickless loser with a twitch?" That's the question. How is it that we end up so far from the perfectly designed person God had in mind for us when we were born?

The people in the *Faithwalking* community suggest that it has something to do with vows we make when we are young. The vows bubble up out of significant life events that happen early on—usually in the form of wounds—that distort the way we look at ourselves and the world for the rest of our lives.

For example, take the classic case of a Depression-era boy raised in the insecurity of grinding poverty who vowed as a child never to be poor again. And from that time on, everything in his life was about finding and maintaining security. "I will be secure" became his vow and that vow formed the deep, often undetectable but nevertheless unrelentingly influential steering current of his life. His whole quest in life was toward security. And then along came Jesus. And Jesus said, *Trust me. Don't store up treasures for yourself on earth, but in heaven. Sell all that you've got and follow Me. Don't worry about your life, what you shall eat or drink or wear but seek first the kingdom of God—TRUST ME.* But the man didn't listen; instead, his vow kicked in and the clouds gathered around Jesus, obscuring His perfect design for the man's life.

Everyone makes vows. Perhaps you can hear the vow in Arnold Schwarzenegger's comment that "Every person I have ever met who has accomplished anything has done it to compensate for some weakness in their life. All my body-building was done to compensate for a sense of inadequacy and weakness in my life at an early age."[1]

You can hear the vow in the words of James Toney, the once World Champion middleweight boxer. He said, "I fight with anger. My Dad, he did my Mother wrong. He made my Mom work two jobs and he left his responsibilities behind and I can never forgive him for that. I hope my father reads this article because if he ever decided to come out of the woodwork, I'll be ready for him. Everything I do is about that. I look at my opponent and I see in his face my Dad and I have to take him out. I'll do anything to get my dad out of him."[2] Can you hear the vow? Can you appreciate how it has directed his life?

You can hear it in what actor Burt Reynolds once said in a *Parade Magazine* interview, "My Dad was chief of police and when he came into a room all the oxygen went out of it. There's a saying in the south that no man is a man until his father tells him he is. It means that someday when you are thirty or forty, this man who you respect and want to love you says to you, 'You're a man now and I love you.' But you know, my Dad never said that to me. We never hugged, never kissed, never said, 'I love you.'" (Reynolds paused and said) "So what happened was that later I was desperately

---

1 Lewis, Robert. *The Quest for Authentic Manhood Bible Study & DVD Pack*. Lifeway: 2004.
2 Ibid.

looking for someone who would say, 'You're grown up, Burt, and I approve of you and I love you and you don't have to do those things anymore.' I was lost inside. I couldn't connect with life. I was incomplete. I didn't know what I needed to know."[3] Can you hear the vow? Can you appreciate how it has directed his life?

In his *The Quest for Authentic Manhood* series, Robert Lewis tells of a man he once met who was raised in embarrassing poverty. At school, he felt the eyes of classmates staring at the rags he wore. One day he stepped out of the run-down trailer his family lived in. He took a few steps away from the cinder-block step, turned around, looked back, and said, "I'm going to get as far away from this trailer as I can." It became his vow. And with that, he set the rudder of his life.

I've got my own vows. My Mother was diagnosed with ovarian cancer a week after her retirement. She and my Dad spent the next sixteen months traveling back and forth to the hospital for various forms of treatment. To pass the time, they listened to public radio and books on tape. One day, they were cleaning out the attic when they came across a box of love letters they had written to each other just before their marriage. So they read these love letters to each other while going for treatments. One of those letters has become one of my most valuable possessions. My mother wrote the letter to my father a couple of weeks before their wedding. In

---

3 Ibid.

it, she acknowledged the brokenness of her family and the pain that her father's selfishness had brought into her world. And then she made a vow, "*Our house is going to be to the children, God first, others second, and themselves last.*" And my mother kept her vow—even to a fault—and in recent years, I have begun to explore how her vow has impacted my life. I know my mother meant nothing but good, but in life there's always the law of unintended consequences. For the most part, I've been grateful for the way her vow introduced into my life the qualities of humility and respectfulness. But the vow she made to my father also unintentionally influenced the way she treated me as a son. In the way she raised me, I sensed through her vow that I was to make myself invisible and avoid calling attention to myself. I know that's not what she said, but it is how I interpreted what she said. After all, in our family it was to be "God first, others second, and me last." I have often puzzled over my strange compulsion not to leave a mark as I move through the world—no footprints in the sand, no marks on the wall, and no echo in the room. So I have felt uncomfortable making phone calls because I know the sound of the telephone will interrupt another's life. Asking others to do things has always made me uncomfortable because, after all, who am I to insert my interests into another's life? Somewhere deep inside of me resides a powerful vow that demands, "I must remain invisible." This vow frequently distorts my response to Jesus' work in my life.

What are your vows?

Choosing new vows that bless

Jesus gives you the perfect view of yourself—but your vows have distorted that view. Even so, the great blessing that comes from studying Jesus is that He begins to free us from bondage to our old vows. Jesus blesses us by helping us choose new, life-giving vows.

It is safe to say that the most important assignment we can accept in life is to keep looking at Jesus, to study Him in search of the blessing He has in mind to give us and the blessing He has in mind for us to be to others.

The Bible announces that:

> *If anyone is in Christ, there is a new creation: everything old*
> *has passed away; see, everything has become new!*
> (2 Corinthians 5:17)

The study of Jesus starts us on the path toward complete transformation. Along the way Jesus never violates our freedom because *love does not insist on its own way.* But Jesus is a master at taking our every movement in His direction and building on it. Jesus doesn't make us change; Jesus helps us change so that at the end of the day, it seems like it was entirely our idea.

The more you study Jesus, the more He infiltrates all the thoughts and systems of your life. He changes the way you look at things, the way you spend your money, the manner of your driving, the style of your conversation, the way you play golf, the way you dress and comb your hair, the way you eat and drink and watch TV. Nothing is off limits. It becomes more and more difficult to determine where you end and Jesus begins.

Beloved, we are God's children now; what we will be has not yet been revealed. What we do know is this: when he is revealed, we will be like him, for we will see him as he is.

(1 John 3:2)

When our daughter Anji was receiving cancer treatments, my wife and I spent a lot of time in the fourth floor waiting area of the Mays Clinic at MD Anderson Cancer Center. Typically, we'd be there for hours. Books, magazines, and jigsaw puzzles were scattered around. To pass the time, we'd take a turn at a puzzle, piecing together a border, a harbor, a barn, a windshield. One day, the only available jigsaw puzzle didn't have a box. The pieces were scattered on the table in a wild display of shapes and colors. Without the picture on the box, no one had had much luck putting the pieces together. To assemble a jigsaw puzzle, you've got to see the picture on the box. And when it comes to transformation, the same is true for you. When you study Jesus, you see the picture of the person you are becoming, but, as with a jigsaw puzzle, the process involves a thousand steps. It's full of trial and error. Sometimes, you'll get stuck. You'll walk away and leave it for a while. Some parts of the puzzle will be easier to assemble than others. The borders and certain distinctive features—like a fence-line or a mailbox—may come together rather quickly like the borders and certain features of the Jesus-life. But the greater challenge of the jigsaw puzzle comes from trying to piece together the larger sections of the puzzle where the picture is less precise and defined. Real life does have a lot of hard-to-define areas. But always remember that by the decree of God, your transformation is unfailing.

To study Jesus is to be launched on a journey of systemic transformation, and as that transformation progresses, blessings begin to flow both into and out of the one being transformed.

CHAPTER ONE

THE BLESSING:
Jesus Goes Slow and Works Small

The central feature of this transformation into the likeness of Jesus is its speed—it is slow, slow, slow! Baby steps. I earlier mentioned my two recent brain surgeries. The second surgery involved disabling part of my balance system. The recovery process has included physical therapy that is designed to reprogram my brain to make up for the loss of balance. For the first few weeks, my progress was measurable, but after that, whatever progress was made was too slow to measure. In fact, on so many occasions, I wondered whether I was making any progress at all. Reprogramming a brain is slow. Reprogramming a life is even slower.

This life-long process of transformation is so gradual that for most of us and for most of the time what we mostly feel is—not much. Except at the beginning. Feelings are usually pretty intense at the beginning of our transformation. Like when I fell in love with Terri. We were sixteen and the experience was overwhelming to me. I couldn't think of anything but her. The mere idea of her affected my pulse, my sleep, my appetite, my study habits. But as the years passed, the intensity of that early passion settled into a quieter and deeper devotion. And now, after more than forty years of marriage, I can say that there isn't a thought that I think, there isn't a decision that I make, there isn't a place that I go that is not influenced by her. My love for her is more influential than ever. Even when I'm not thinking of her, I'm thinking of her. She is the chief human influence in my life.

Blessings in the slow lane

How strange that transformation into the likeness of Jesus impacts every area of life and yet it is generally undetectable. For this reason, we are often left with the impression that nothing much is happening. Jesus once described the work of the Kingdom of God as a seed growing secretly. We are changing, but much of the time, the change is a secret even to us. Dale Bruner refers to Charles Erdman's Law that "The one who is most filled with the Spirit is the one who is least aware of it. All they know is that they love Jesus and want to serve Him." Without really knowing it, you begin to agree with what Paul wrote:

...it is no longer I who live, but it is Christ who lives in me. And the life I now live in the flesh I live by faith in the Son of God, who loved me and gave himself for me.

(Galatians 2:20)

I think the Spirit of Christ works in us like an electrical transformer. Transformers come in all sizes. The Grand Coulee Dam on the Columbia River in central Washington State is the largest concrete structure and largest generator of electrical power in the United States. It generates 6,809 megawatts of power. A megawatt is equivalent to one million watts. Do the math and you get the idea that Grand Coulee Dam generates enormous electrical power. The force of such electrical power would most certainly vaporize you if you came in contact with the whole of it. When I lived near the dam in Eastern Washington, I used to touch the electrical connection that I used to charge my computer. I would plug it into the wall and touch the outlet and I wouldn't feel a thing—not even the slightest buzz of electrical shock. It was connected to the vast vaporizing source of power in the Grand Coulee Dam, and yet somehow when I plugged the electrical cord into that wall outlet, I couldn't feel a thing. How was that possible? Transformers. Transformers translate the vast power of Grand Coulee Dam into units of power that are useful in my life—from the air conditioner, to the dishwasher, to the yard light, to the hair dryer, to the computer charger.

The Spirit of Christ works in a similar way, transforming the vast power of God into useful units of energy in your life that allow you to behave like Him, but without being vaporized by the encounter. Most of the time, you don't feel "shocked" by encounters with Jesus; you simply find yourself doing the things Jesus does—you find yourself empowered—transformed.

These useful units of power that the Spirit of Christ releases into our lives are described in the Bible in these ways:

Compassion, kindness, humility, meekness, and patience. Bear with one another…forgive one other…let the peace of Christ rule in your hearts…let the word of Christ dwell in you richly.
(Colossians 3:12-17)

The peace of God, which surpasses all understanding, will guard your hearts and your minds in Christ Jesus…
Whatever is true, honorable, just, pure, pleasing, commendable, excellent.…anything worthy of praise, think about these things. Keep on doing the things that you have learned and received and heard and seen in me, and the God of peace will be with you.
(Philippians 4:4-9)

Love is patient; love is kind; love is not envious or boastful or arrogant or rude. It does not insist on its own way; it is not irritable or resentful; it does not rejoice in wrongdoing, but rejoices in the truth. It bears all things, believes all things, hopes all things, endures all things. Love never ends.
(1 Corinthians 13:4-7)

Each of these qualities and many more like them that are described in scripture are the useful units of transformational energy that the indwelling Spirit of Jesus brings to life in us.

And if you are willing, they will produce gradual change in you.

Because *love does not insist on its own way,* the Spirit of God will not force you to do anything you don't want to do, but if you choose to live as God commands, His Spirit will empower you to act. And furthermore, the Spirit of God will empower you so gently that it will often feel as if you did it in your own strength.

To "study Jesus" means keeping connected to Him through prayer, Bible study, and fellowship. It means leaning your life in His direction. You can lean toward Jesus even while you're doing other things. You can drive your car while leaning toward Jesus. You can make business deals while leaning toward Jesu. You can play tennis, hit golf balls, fly-fish in a river while leaning toward Jesus. You can argue with your spouse, debate with the IRS, talk to your doctor, and at the same time, lean toward Jesus. You can pay your bills, do the laundry, iron shirts, pull weeds, read a book, watch TV, and at the same time, lean toward Jesus. And the more you honor Him in this way, the more your life becomes His life. Eugene Peterson, renowned scholar, pastor, and author of the bestselling paraphrase of the Bible, *The Message,* describes it as, "A long obedience in the same direction." But it is slow!

Blessings "on second thought"

The Jesus-life transformation goes slowly partly because it's difficult to understand and partly because it's difficult to do. Since our original wiring is not sympathetic to the Jesus-life, it requires us to go against our natural sensibilities and desires. The journey to Christ-likeness is all upstream, all uphill.

After my brain surgery, physical therapy was a new experience for me. I realized fairly quickly that my physical therapist's strategy was to figure out what I couldn't do and then make me do it over and over again until I gained some strength and proficiency. Jesus is our therapist. He's an expert at identifying the places where our lives are out of balance and making us do those things until we gain proficiency.

Faithfulness is rarely if ever our first thought. Since it's not our first nature, faithfulness will always be "on second thought," or third, or fourth, or fiftieth.

And every step of progress in the Jesus-life is entirely voluntary. Jesus will not force you to do anything you don't want to do because, *Love does not insist on its own way.*

Take just one small example: We live in such a visually provocative culture. By original design, we are pre-wired to notice each other. The challenge is to notice without sinning. When does noticing edge toward sinning? In teaching about adultery, Jesus said:

If your right eye causes you to sin, pluck it out and throw it away; it's better to go through life blind than to be thrown into the hell of fire.

(Mark 5:29)

Dale Bruner says we enter the danger zone when we look a second time. The first look is free. The first look is in our nature. Trouble comes when we look a second time. But here's the challenge. It is in our human nature to look again—and again. And it's such a small thing—learning not to look a second time. But progress toward holiness comes in baby steps like these—looking once, but not twice. No one else notices, but Jesus cheers when we refuse to look a second time.

This slow movement toward faithfulness is repeated over and over and over again in every area and arena of life.

Progress is slow and difficult and entirely voluntary—a little at a time—slow and small—by degrees.

And all of us, with unveiled faces, seeing the glory of the Lord as though reflected in a mirror, are being transformed into the same image from one degree of glory to another; for this comes from the Lord, the Spirit.

(2 Corinthians 3:18)

There are 360 degrees on a directional compass. The difference between each degree is so slight you can hardly tell one from the next. And yet, if you were to fly from the East

Coast to the West, a tiny, imperceptible, one-degree change in direction could spell the difference between arriving in Los Angeles or in Seattle. The transformation of our lives is, similarly, by degrees. We complain that our Christian progress seems so slow. But God knows that little changes are being made that we hardly notice, but that dramatically alter our final destination. We may not yet be what we long to be, but, by studying Jesus, neither are we what we used to be.

Malcolm Gladwell studied exceptional people—"outliers" he called them. People who in various fields and disciplines are exceptional. He was searching for common denominators. In his book *Outliers: The Story of Success*, he described several, including "The Ten-Thousand Hour Rule." Dedicating yourself to learning or practicing something for twenty hours a week for ten years produces an exceptional outcome. Joshua Foer discovered the same thing in his own life. He got interested in the World Memory Championships. He assumed competitors were naturally gifted. He discovered that memory is more a discipline than a gift. In his book *Moonwalking with Einstein: The Art and Science of Remembering Everything*, Foer applied the principle of the ten-thousand hour rule for a year and actually won the United States Memory Championship.

I've boiled down the three great obstacles to my own transformation to the three "Cs" of Comfort, Control, and Consumption. I love being comfortable, I thrive in an environment where I maintain control, and I tend to want what I want when I want it. My quest to maintain my three C's presents a constant impediment to my growth. These desires are so deeply rooted in me, they have infected every decision I make.

The South Pacific contains something like 10,000 islands. During World War II, the Allies had to fight battles on every island to win them back. That's what my life is like. Comfort, control, and consumption have invaded every island of my life, and the battle for transformation involves little battles for liberation on 10,000 beachheads. So progress is slow and the steps are small.

But the amazing truth is that if you work, God will work in you. And at the end of the day, it will seem to you as if you chose to do it and you did it in your own strength, when in fact, it was Christ being "transformed" into your life.

...work out your own salvation with fear and trembling; for it is God who is at work in you, enabling you both to will and to work for his good pleasure.

(Philippians 2:12-13)

CHAPTER TWO

THE APPLICATION:
Go Slow and Small with Others

You will bless others by appreciating the speed and size of their transformation. Impatience is the enemy of blessing. When it comes to transformation in others, you bless them by not being in a hurry.

The slow pace can become discouraging. And discouragement can be lethal. Sometimes, people just need to hear someone say, "You've got it in you. You can do it. Don't give up. Keep going." Everyone wonders why his or her own transformation takes so long. That's why the saying, "Three steps forward two steps back" never goes out of style.

When blessings come slowly

When people's progress seems slow, notice their little acts of progress, and cheer them on.

As I've said regarding the reprogramming of my brain, I've figured out that the objective of my physical therapist is to find out what I can't do and then to make me do it—over and over again. And the thing is, because I can't do it, I always feel stupid—and feeling stupid is my least favorite feeling. I get my therapy at the Texas Institute for Rehabilitation and Research. One day my physical therapist, Michael, had me stand heel-to-toe on a yellow line, moving my head back and forth while staring at a capital E that he had taped to the wall. It's really the simplest exercise. Any normal person could do it. But there I was with my calf muscles burning and my toes digging into the concrete to keep from toppling over. I made five turns of my head in ten seconds before tipping to the side. Michael caught me and sent up a cheer. It felt like total failure to me. It was the simplest move, but he recognized the difficulty of it for a person in my condition, and he reminded me that a month before, that move had been impossible for me. I appreciate that Michael is not in a hurry for my transformation. I am grateful that he points out my progress, especially when it's slow.

Impatience is the enemy of blessing. There's nothing quick about transformation. It's slow and involves sustained effort in the same direction over the long haul. And it turns out that the slow speed of the transformation is also part of the blessing. Jesus is never in a hurry. He understands the complexity of the process. He appreciates, far better than we, how long it takes. What may appear to be a minor piece of progress to us is often a major accomplishment to Jesus. For a child, "firsts" are big—first steps, first words, first visits to the potty, first days at school. And each "first" is accompanied by loud applause and celebration. But when you get older, no one cheers when you take a step, speak a word, or emerge from the restroom. What starts out as epic accomplishment becomes routine. Believe me, Jesus never stops cheering each tiny bit of progress, even though to us progress seems slight and the speed seems slow.

When falling and failing block blessings

When people around you fall and fail, help them get back up again. The world loves to discredit and discard people in failure. During one recent Olympic competition in one of the women's ski events, one contestant missed a gate. She didn't fall; she just missed the gate. To her credit, rather than quit, she slowly made her way back up the course to ski through the gate and to the finish line. When she crossed the line, she was obviously deflated. She still had one more run, but she was also fourteen seconds behind. In an event where the difference between medals and no medals is tenths of a second, fourteen seconds was an eternity. Somehow, the camera found her mother in the crowd. Their eyes met and I could read her mother's lips as she shouted encouragement. The daughter's lips complained, "But Mom, it's fourteen seconds!" But there was one more run, and you never know what might happen, and her mom shouted, "It's okay! You can do it!" Keep encouraging others. It's a blessing toward transformation. Sometimes, people just need to be reminded what's in them.

When blessings require you to turn around

When people are lost and heading the wrong way, help them turn around. I was waiting for a light to change at a busy intersection. The window in the car next to me rolled down and the face of a confused woman appeared. She motioned to me to roll down my window, so I did. She asked, "How do I get to the Sam Houston Tollway?" I glanced up and noticed that the traffic light in the other direction had just changed to yellow and that meant our light was about to turn green. I had the time it takes for the light to turn from yellow to green to give this woman directions to the Sam Houston Tollway. So I hollered out the window, "Turn around on this road, keep going, don't give up, and you'll get there." It's good advice for others.

You bless people when you help them turn around and choose a better destination. Remind people that it's never where you are that matters. It's where you're headed. In Jesus' story of the Prodigal Son, the father ran to meet the son, not when he managed to escape the far country, but rather, in the moment he turned around in the far country.

When pressures take the focus off blessings

When the pressure is on and focus is difficult, remind others of the important things. At the Olympic swimming and diving trials, divers climbed the ten-meter platform to do their best. Ten meters is higher than a three-story building.

In the women's diving competition, I noticed that before each diver launched into thin air, she paused and seemed to speak to someone, but there was no one anywhere around. I was curious. And then, as if to answer my unspoken question, the commentator said, "You may notice how each diver pauses and seems to speak before competing. In case you are wondering, they are repeating out loud the last words their coach told them."

Discouragement and disillusionment haunt our progress. Three questions can help keep moving people forward with hopeful anticipation.

What happened?

What did you learn?

What will you do next time?

It's never so much a matter of where we are that matters but where we are headed. These questions help us calculate location and plot trajectory.

Our natural wiring is for speed and progress. We'd prefer for the Jesus-life to be something we can complete like a college degree so we can move on to other things in life. But it doesn't work that way. At the annual examination of candidates for ministry, after all the questions about the Bible and theology, an old pastor in the back of the church would always ask Frank Harrington, pastor of the Peachtree

Presbyterian Church, "So Frank, have you made any progress in your daily walk with Jesus?" And this walk is longer and harder than anyone expects.

As I mentioned earlier, three days after my brain surgery, my head was still in an unrelenting and nightmarish spin. I couldn't walk. In fact, I could just barely even sit up in bed. I was feeling desperate when my surgeon appeared. He sat on the bed and encouraged me. In fact, he got Terri on the phone and he announced, "Terri, he's golden!" Well, at that moment I was anything but golden, but I'll never forget his words. He was announcing what would be true for me long before it was.

The Spirit of Jesus is at work in people who trust their lives to His care. Progress is slow and small, but it is happening, and one day, it will be complete. So:

Do all things without murmuring and arguing, so that you may be blameless and innocent, children of God without blemish in the midst of a crooked and perverse generation, in which you shine like stars in the world.
(Philippians 2:14-15)

DIALOGUE BOX

Your journal

Who have been role models for you in your life? How have these people shaped the person you have become?

Your prayers

Consider the places where you habitually resist transformation. Confess these to God and give Him permission to work in those areas.

Your discussion

- Think over your life and identify and describe places where you see subtle transformation taking place in you.

- In what ways do others' tedious transformations aggravate you? How do you respond to their slow progress?

Your memory

2 Corinthians 3:17-18

Your action

- Identify a new behavior you'd like to adopt. What steps can you take to turn this behavior into a habit?

- Ask someone to join you in a growth-accountability friendship where you support each other in transformational change.

CHAPTER THREE

THE BLESSING:
Jesus is Warm and Approachable

Studying Jesus blesses us by giving us an idea of who He is and who we are becoming. Of all the people who have ever lived, Jesus is most shockingly warm and approachable. When you study Jesus' life, you can't help but be struck by the intensity of His sensitivity to wounded, broken, and needy people. And His sensitivity produced a deeply heartfelt response. Take for instance this encounter:

One of the Pharisees asked Jesus to eat with him, and he went into the Pharisee's house and took his place at the table. And a woman in the city, who was a sinner, having learned that he was eating in the Pharisee's house, brought an alabaster jar of ointment. She stood behind him at his feet, weeping, and began to bathe his feet with her tears and to dry them with her hair. Then she continued kissing his feet and anointing them with the ointment.
(Luke 7:36-38)

Her response to Jesus defied every social rule. She approached Jesus without being invited, she let down her hair in public, she wept over Him, and she washed His feet with her hair. Each of these actions would have been explicitly forbidden in the first century Hebrew edition of Emily Post's book of etiquette. What would provoke this woman to behave this way? Was it Jesus' great mind? Was it His extraordinary power? Was it His deep wisdom? While each of these qualities was impressive, it was really the warmth of His humanity that moved this woman and the world.

A blessing greater than signs and wonders

More than Jesus' commanding Presence, His brilliant mind and exceptional power—calming the sea and casting out demons and raising the dead—it's His warmth, humility, and humanity that exposes Him. The way He laid aside His Divine power and authority and humbled Himself to life on earth and death on a cross—that is how He exposed the heart of God. Jesus never owned anything except the clothes on His back and the substance of His personality. We read a lot about His signs and wonders, His brilliant intellect. It's good to know Jesus in these ways. But when you follow Jesus through the New Testament, you keep encountering people who follow Him with tears in their eyes.

Jesus had a way of approaching people and of touching them with such light and warmth that healing came to their bodies and tears to their eyes. The prophet Isaiah described Jesus perfectly when he said:

A bruised reed he will not break,
and a dimly burning wick he will not quench.
(Isaiah 42:3)

If you've ever walked in a marsh in the autumn of the year, you know about bruised reeds. With the slightest touch they collapse. And you can picture a dimly burning wick and how just the slightest movement of air will extinguish its flame. Jesus personified such warmth and gentleness that bruised reeds and dimly burning wicks were safe in His Presence.

It's much more than His being simply "gentle" or "nice." With Jesus, it is His Presence. He is with us, and not just in the sense of accompanying us, but experiencing life with us—as though our life were actually His life. In the movie *Absolute Power*, Clint Eastwood was estranged from his daughter, Laura Linney. When a police detective, Ed Harris, came looking for Eastwood, his daughter announced, "I don't know where he is. I haven't seen him in years. I have no relationship with him. I don't even know where he lives." The detective said, "I know where he lives." And he took her there. He found a door key under a flowerpot and let them in. Her eyes slowly adjusted to the dimly filtered light. All around the living room, she saw photos of herself. In the kitchen, the bedroom, the hallways—everywhere it was the same—photos of her in all the places she'd been, as an infant, as a child, as a girl, as a young woman. At school, at play, at work. Big moments and little. At first she stammered, "This isn't possible; he wasn't in these places." And then she half-whispered, "It's strange; I always felt that he was there."

The thing about Jesus is that He's always been there—in every place you've been. He knows what you've gained and what you've lost, how you've rejoiced and how you've wept. He's dreamed your fantasies and your nightmares. He hasn't just watched you—He's lived with you in those moments. He has been with you. He has been in you.

And after all these years, what He feels for you is a warmth of affection that is unfathomable.

For years, Les and Cindy Morgan served as medical missionaries in Bangladesh. But when their twenty-year-old son Everett contracted cancer, they came to Houston to concentrate on his treatments. As the year passed, despite every therapeutic effort, their son's life slipped away. There is no grief like a parent for a child. Someone gave Cindy a small replica of Michelangelo's Pieta. That image of a mother tenderly holding the broken body of her son became a great source of comfort to her. It was the comfort that can only come from knowing another at the deepest level. Les and Cindy came to know the warmth of Jesus' compassion and approachableness with tears in their eyes.

Let Jesus speak for Himself:

Come to me, all you that are weary and are carrying heavy burdens, and I will give you rest. Take my yoke upon you, and learn from me; for I am gentle and humble in heart, and you will find rest for your souls. For my yoke is easy, and my burden is light.

(Matthew 11:28-30)

Love blesses even in the shadows

More often than I would like to remember, I have been summoned into circles where suicide has taken a life. Minds strain to understand why. Survivors implore me for assurances that God will not reject the one they have loved and lost. God throws Psalm 34:18 to us like a lifeline:

The Lord is near to the broken-hearted, and saves the crushed in spirit.

Terri and I first started dating when we were sixteen. Her family had a rule that we could only see each other on weekend evenings. I had a job bagging groceries, and one evening, I just felt compelled to see her on my way home. Her bedroom was on the lower level. I parked my car on the street, crept through the gardens, and came to her window. The curtains were drawn, but I could see her dim shadow reflected in the lamplight of her desk. I tapped quietly on the window. Her shadow sat up. I tapped again; her shadow turned slowly toward the window. I tapped again. She stepped to the window and yanked the curtains open. It was pitch black outside as I stood there, hidden almost entirely in the shadows. It was her bloodcurdling scream that suggested my plan had lacked a certain forethought. I did my best to exude the fullness of the warmth of love I felt for her, but sometimes, it's hard to recognize love when it's hidden in the shadows.

We live in a world of shadows. As you study Jesus, you begin to see Him moving in the painful, terrifying, confusing shadows of life. And you realize in the shadows of life that the power at the center of the universe has drawn near to the brokenhearted to save those crushed in spirit.

The power at the center of the universe moves through the marsh of humanity's bruised reeds and dimly burning wicks with a gentleness of character that does not break us but heals us, does not extinguish us, but increases the flame of our life. The power at the center of the universe is warm and approachable. Study Jesus and you will receive this blessing.

CHAPTER FOUR

THE APPLICATION:
Be Warm and Approachable
with Others

Like Jesus, you were designed to be warm and approachable. When we study Jesus with the understanding that He is our model, we begin to grasp a sense of the potential we contain to be similarly warm and approachable. The world cries in desperation for us to bless it in this way. As Jesus said:

> *By this everyone will know that you are my disciples, if you have love for one another.*
> (John 13:35)

Everything we aspire to do with our heart, Jesus says, "Do it with love." With all we aspire to do with our mind, Jesus says, "Do it with love." With all that we aspire to do with our soul, Jesus says, "Do it with love." With all that we aspire to do with our strength, Jesus says, "Do it with love." There is nothing emptier than accomplishment without love.

Wounds and breaks cry for blessing

Try to understand that every person you meet is wounded and broken. We carry our woundedness in so many unpleasant and abrasive ways. A thirteen-year-old girl in a church where I once served was in a terrible automobile accident. Her leg was severed, but it was then surgically reattached. As you can imagine, she spent months in the hospital enduring multiple surgeries and endless sessions of physical therapy. When I visited her a day or two before her release, she asked whether I wanted to see her leg. To be honest, I didn't feel the need to, but she seemed to need to show me. When she pulled back the dressings, I was appalled to see that, after all these months, there was still a gaping hole and a wound that was large and open. She could see my alarm. She explained, "They tell me that a wound this deep has to heal from the inside out."

We all carry concealed wounds. Every person you have ever known is healing from the inside out. Most of the trouble we see in the world comes from the crippling effect and the putrid stench of our unhealed hidden wounds. Everything you see in others that appalls, annoys, and offends you comes from unhealed wounds—theirs and yours. And the smelly complications of our brokenness constantly derail our life in community.

But God has blessed you with His own astonishing gentleness, and He intends for you to bless others by being warm and approachable—by walking like Jesus did through the marshes of bruised humanity and dimly burning wicks. To paraphrase the Bible:

Love one another. Encourage one another. Forgive one another. Outdo one another in showing honor. Bless and do not curse.

To the extent it is possible for you, exude warmth and mercy, kindness and approachability into your relationships.

Blaine Williams is a member of the church where I serve. Complications occurred with Blaine's birth so he's spent his life managing various physical limitations. But beyond these limitations, Blaine is one of the wisest and most remarkable people I know, and one of the most authentically Christian. One day, the rear doors of the sanctuary opened while I was speaking. In rolled Blaine. His chair was positioned next to a wheelchair occupied by Nicholas. Nicholas is blind and deaf. He has never spoken to anyone, never been able to care for himself. His parents, Michelle and Francisco, had heroically devoted their lives to their son's needs. Because of the severity of Nicholas' limitations, it's impossible for most people to know how to respond to him. But when Blaine's chair rolled to a stop beside Nicholas' chair, he gently and quietly reached out and took his hand. And it was so beautiful. It was so perfect. It was so warm and gentle. It was so Christ-like. An hour later, Michelle was still overcome! A year later, she still had tears in her eyes.

The whole world groans for this—to make loving contact with others. The distortion of this need lies behind every human problem. The fulfillment of this need stands behind every healing.

You are the symphonic reduction of Jesus' blessings

A young man stood in our kitchen explaining his life story. He described his parents' painful divorce, the quiet and nearly suffocating loneliness and fear he felt growing up. Worst of all was his estrangement from his father. He paused and said with cloudy eyes, "I'm thirty-two years old and even still, every time the telephone rings on my birthday, I dream it is my father calling to tell me happy birthday and he loves me—but he never calls."

That pain or a variation of it can be found in every person you will ever meet.

How will the world know you are Jesus' disciples? Not by your intellect, not your power, not your cleverness, your business acumen, the strength of your serve, the length of your drive, the eloquence of your tongue—none of these will bless others—but rather it will be by the warmth of your humanity and goodwill.

You were designed by God to reflect Jesus' warmth and gentleness into the world. As our choir was preparing to sing its anthem, Dr. Charles Hausmann, our music director, commented that normally this particular piece of music would be accompanied by a full orchestra, but since that was impractical on this occasion, he had substituted the full orchestra with a "symphonic reduction," and he turned and pointed to a solo violinist on the stage. She was the symphonic reduction. With her violin, she replaced 100 orchestral instruments—the strings, percussion, brass, and woodwinds. The whole 100-piece orchestra was summed up in her single violin. By your love and warmth, you are the symphonic reduction of Jesus.

Study Jesus and you see that the summary of God is that His unfailing love for us makes Him warm and approachable. Study Jesus and you will see that the summary of your purpose in life is to be warm and approachable.

DIALOGUE BOX

Your journal

> What were the most painful moments of your child-hood?

Your prayers

> Ask Jesus to help you see how these events have dis-torted your life as an adult.

Your discussion

- How do you respond to others' pain and brokenness?

- Listen to the stories other group members tell. Express to them what you believe Jesus would say to them.

Your memory

> Psalm 34:18

Your action

- Make a list of three annoying habits you see in others and develop a warm and gracious response to each.

CHAPTER FIVE

THE BLESSING:
Jesus is Faithful and Just

Jesus' warmth and approachability are only half of the story. The other half is His brilliance in doing justice. Nothing was more unique or unsettling about Jesus than the way He did justice. Jesus filled the law full—with love. In this way, He "full-filled" it. He is justice with a heart. In Jesus, we see the perfect balance between love and justice, between grace and truth, between conviction and compassion.

Do not think that I have come to abolish the law or the prophets; I have come not to abolish but to fulfill.
(Matthew 5:17)

One of my greatest struggles in life is finding the balance between law and love, between conviction and compassion. I don't want to be overly-permissive; neither do I want to be overly-legalistic. My goal is holding the balance between the two. The danger of drifting to either side makes me think of Annie Dillard's experience while staring into the waters of Tinker Creek in the Blue Ridge Mountains of Virginia. For a year, she studied the world and kept a journal on solitude, writing, religion, and creation. Her book, *Pilgrim at Tinker Creek,* won the Pulitzer Prize. It's a magical celebration of creation. She once sat staring at a frog floating in the creek. While she watched, the frog slowly collapsed into itself, deflating like a balloon losing its air. Its skin just sagged and its eyes turned cloudy and lifeless. Then, from just beneath the frog, a dark shadow moved away. It was a water beetle. With silent stealth, it had drifted under the frog, inserted its straw-like mouth into the underside of the frog, and sucked the life right out of it.

No one wants his convictions to suck the life out of his compassion. No one wants his love to deflate the importance of the law. Jesus kept the perfect balance between the two. Jesus fully embraced the law, and through it, He demonstrated His hatred of sin and all its deadly consequences.

Jesus blesses justice by hating sin

To catch the intensity of this balance, read Jesus' Sermon on the Mount in Matthew 5, 6, and 7. As one sample, listen to what Jesus said about the way we should respond to our sinful tendencies:

> *If your right eye causes you to sin, tear it out and throw it away; it is better for you to lose one of your members than for your whole body to be thrown into hell. And if your right hand causes you to sin, cut it off and throw it away; it is better*

for you to lose one of your members than for your whole body
to go into hell.
(Matthew 5:29-30)

"Pluck out your eye...cut off your arm..." It's hard to imagine being more emphatic in emphasizing the urgency of a devout and holy life. In His own life, Jesus carried a deep resolve for holiness, purity, and obedience to God's Law. No one ever lived a more moral and obedient life than Jesus. Jesus is the epitome of legalism. The Bible tells us that in His life, Jesus faced every form of sin and resisted. It's incomprehensible to imagine facing every form of sin and resisting.

The default position for the rest of us is to be "pretty good" or "good enough" or perhaps a few clicks better than average. Lewis Smedes captured this reality in his book, *A Pretty Good Person.* Smedes explored the enormous challenge of fully living up to the standard of God's law. Our tendency is to wink at sin. To be philosophical about our fallen state. We make an easy peace with the routine forms of everyday sin. One evening, Terri and I were cleaning up after dinner. Television programming transitioned over from the evening news to the first sitcom. I wasn't familiar with the show, but in the first five minutes, there were three or four examples of what can only be described as blatantly sinful behavior—and it came with a laugh-track. But sin is no laughing matter. If you follow the course of every sin, no matter how large or small, it will eventually lead to tragedy. So Jesus did more than settle for "pretty good" and "good enough." Jesus' standard was perfection.

This sin-free life seems impossible because some temptations are so irresistible. As hard as we try, we CAN'T say no. The harder we try to resist, the more compelling the temptation becomes. No one stated it any better than St. Paul:

> *I do not understand my own actions. For I do not do what I want, but I do the very thing I hate.*
> (Romans 7:15)

It's impossible to live a sin-free day, a sin free hour, or a sin-free minute. Sin knows how to push our buttons and control our behavior. If you want to appreciate the heroic dimension of Jesus' resistance of sin, just try to live a sin-free life.

And it's also impossible because some temptations are so subtle we scarcely know what we're doing even when we sin. The sin before us takes many disguises. The Arbinger Institute leads the field in exploring the problem of self-deception. In its book, *Leadership and Self-Deception*, the institute recounts that story of Ignaz Semmelweis, a researcher and physician at Vienna General Hospital in the mid-1800s. He divided his time between research in the lab working on cadavers, and delivering babies in the maternity ward. His particular area of concern was the high mortality rate of mothers in his maternity ward where 1 in 10 died after giving birth. The cause was mysterious, but it struck terror into mothers who came to Vienna General to give birth. Many chose instead to have their babies out on the street. After years of dead-end research, Dr. Semmelweis took a sabbatical to study the experience in other hospitals. He was surprised to discover that the mortality rate in other hospitals was much lower—more like 1 in 50. Still baffled, he returned to Vienna General only to discover that in his absence, the mortality rate had improved significantly. Gradually, it occurred to him that perhaps somehow HE might be the cause. And in time, he developed a theory that perhaps he was transferring deadly microbes from the cadavers in the lab to the moms in the maternity ward. This was in the days before there was any clear understanding of germs. But as soon as Dr. Semmelweis began washing his hands after working on cadavers, the morality rate improved dramatically. Then Dr. Semmelweis had to face the tragic irony that at the very time he thought he was giving life, he was actually administering death.

Dr. Semmelweis is the poster child for what is known as the power of self-deception. The subtle nature of sin makes us all vulnerable to self-deception. We are often not aware that our convictions lay a veneer of deception over our sin.

A man once explained to me with the greatest conviction that he was justified in leaving his wife for another married woman because of the love God had given them for each other. Sin even hides behind the self-deceiving illusion of love.

How did Jesus do it? How did he live a sin-free life? Jesus spoke with crystal clarity about His tactic. He trusted the Word of His Heavenly Father completely. He maneuvered the bewildering labyrinth of sinful temptation by His resolute and faithful obedience to scripture. Similarly, our best and only hope is to trust and obey the Word God gives us. Some elements of it will make perfect sense, some will be baffling, and others will seem downright irrational. That's why Paul said:

We walk by faith, not sight.
(2 Corinthians 5:17)

Conventional wisdom says, "Think for yourself." Jesus teaches that when we trust God, our IQ increases. We are never smarter than when we trust God's Word.

It feels strange to say that we are to "hate" anything. Even so, for Jesus the first part of doing justice was to hate sin because of the ways that in every form and every size and on every scale it kills, steals, and destroys.

Jesus blesses justice by becoming a fountain of grace to sinners

It's certainly true that Jesus hates sin, but He also personifies justice by offering Himself as a fountain of grace to sinners.

1. Jesus graces us with time to think. When the religious leaders brought the adulterous woman to Jesus and asked Him what they should do with her (John 8), instead of offering a quick answer Jesus knelt down and wrote on the ground while they peppered Him with accusatory questions. Jesus opened up a reflective space for them by not immediately engaging the question. The capacity for reflection is one of the most unique and distinguishing features of being human. Most of what we know best we know because we've thought about it for years. How often have our first responses been the wrong responses? How often has our own sinfulness seized the advantage by causing us to respond without thinking? How often have we lived to regret the impulsive and thoughtless response? How often would we have been better to wait an hour or a day or a week?

2. Jesus graces us by not condemning. Jesus condemned neither the religious leaders nor the woman caught in adultery. To the leaders, He invited self-examination. John says that Jesus:

> *...knew all people and needed no one to testify about anyone;*
> *for He Himself knew what was in everyone.*
> (John 2:24-5)

And yet even though He knew the dark inner world of these religious leaders, Jesus did not point out their sins. Jesus graciously invited them to engage in their own self-examination.

Neither did Jesus condemn the woman.

> *Neither do I condemn you.*
> *Go your way, and from now on do not sin again.*
> (John 8:11)

We don't know any more of this woman's story. We don't know whether she was so impacted by Jesus' blessing that she lived forever-after a holy, devout, and transformed life or whether she drifted back to her old sinful ways. We don't know whether she joyfully accepted Jesus' release from her dark past or she just limped through the rest of her days plagued by guilt and shame. What we do know is that Jesus did not condemn her.

3. Jesus resists condemnation. On several occasions, Jesus insisted that He came NOT to condemn. Once, when being questioned by religious officials, Jesus offered this explanation:

> *The one who rejects me and does not receive my word has a*
> *judge; on the last day the word that I have spoken will serve as*
> *judge, for I have not spoken on my own, but the Father who*
> *sent me has himself given me a commandment about what to*
> *say and what to speak.*
> (John 12:48-49)

For a long time, I was baffled by the meaning of these words. And then an old memory brought understanding. As a boy, my parents told me over and over not to ride my bike through the stop sign at the intersection of Reese Road and Sunset Drive. But there was never much traffic on Reese Road so I couldn't imagine the harm in it. Until one fateful day. The next thing I knew, I was lying on the street next to my mangled bike with a bumper of the car that had just struck me looming just over my head. My terrified parents gathered me up in their arms and carried me to the couch. They put ice on my bruised and bloodied leg and spoke to me gently. No one ever even whispered, "We told you so." After all, what was the use in that? They didn't have to. I could hear, ringing in my ears, their thousand words of warning from the past. I kept wishing I'd listened. At that moment, their role was not to condemn, but to comfort and restore.

I think that's what Jesus meant when He said, "I do not judge; the word that I have spoken will serve as judge." Before we fall, Jesus speaks clearly the word of Law. But after we fall, He becomes a fountain of grace to restore us again.

The more immediate question is: What do we do with Jesus' blessing? How do we respond to the fountain of His grace?

Doing justice is one of humanity's most perplexing challenges. Judging sinners without becoming judgmental, condemning sin without becoming condemning, hating sin without hating sinners is enormously difficult. Jesus personifies justice by hating sin while at the same time showering sinners in a fountain of grace. What a blessing.

CHAPTER SIX

THE APPLICATION:
Be Faithful and Just with Others

You bless the world when you follow Jesus' example of living justly, but as Jesus shows us, justice is far more complex and life-giving than simply keeping rules.

Bless justice by hating sin

Living justly begins with a deep understanding of the nature of sin. What is sin? Sin gets a lot of attention in scripture. Over history, people have developed biblical lists of the Seven Deadly Sins: pride, gluttony, greed, envy, sloth, lust, and wrath. Sin is often described as separation from God. Some people have described sin as failure to trust God's love. You might think of sin as anything that lowers God's standard of living.

In the Bible, *sin* is often expressed using three descriptive terms—*Sin, Trespass,* and *Debt.* It helps to look at each word.

1. Understanding Sin. The word sin originated in the world of archery. When an arrow is fired at a target, if it comes up short or goes too long, it is called a sin—meaning "to miss the mark." In this sense, sin is the failure to be in the place you are supposed to be.

Not long ago, I had a memorial service scheduled for 2 p.m. My calendar of morning responsibilities ended at 11 a.m. and I was grateful to have the three hours between 11 and 2 to make final preparations for the memorial service. I needed to run a quick errand and was away from the building until about 11:07. When I drove into the parking lot, my assistant, Gena, was waving her arms in some kind of distress. She shouted, "The memorial service—it's NOW." Somehow, without my knowing, the service had been rescheduled from 2 p.m. to 11 a.m. The chapel was full, the music was playing, the friends had gathered and there I was in the parking lot without my tie, without my robe, and most importantly, without my message. In forty years of ministry and 12,000 speaking engagements, I had never been late for anything. It was my worst nightmare. I was not in the place I was supposed to be. One dimension of sin is the failure to be where we are supposed to be.

And we can fail to be where we're supposed to be in many, many different ways. The failure may be physical, emotional, intellectual, spiritual, or relational.

2. Understanding Trespass. The word *trespass* is, in some respects, self-explanatory. To trespass means to be in a place we're not supposed to be. Our home in Spokane, Washington sat at the base of Browne's Mountain. It was

really a minimal mountain a little more than 4,000 feet high
and only about 2,000 feet higher than the elevation of our
home. At the time, our two sons were young and adven-
turesome in spirit. Together, we'd daydream about climbing Browne's Mountain. So one day we did. Like Lewis
and Clark, Kevin, Grant, and I set off up the mountain.
We followed a dirt road about halfway up until we were
confronted by a large steel gate crowned with barbed wire
and surrounded with stern NO TRESPASSING signs. It
seems that the top of the mountain was covered with sensitive communication towers. And what were we to do? We
had come so far. We had dreamed so long. We had prepared
so well. We had water and lunch in our backpacks. While
my sons stared at me, I gave it some thought and then made
an executive decision. We'd squeeze through a narrow opening between the gate and the fence and continue climbing
toward the top. But from the moment we squeezed through,
there was no more pleasure in the climb. We no longer followed the road. Instead, we battled through the thick un-
derbrush, being careful not to be seen trespassing. Every
sound sent us into hiding. A helicopter approached and we
were sure we'd been spotted. Eventually, we made the top of
the mountain, but the view was hard to enjoy because we
were confined to our hiding places. We couldn't even enjoy
our lunch. We were, after all, trespassing. We were in a place
we should not have been.

Life often presents us with opportunities to go where we should not. And those places may be physical, emotional, intellectual, spiritual, or relational.

3. Understanding Debt. Penalties exist for failing to be in places we should be and for being in places we shouldn't, and the penalties put us in *debt* to God. In fact, by the Bible's account, these debts accumulate to a level that far exceeds our ability to pay. To illustrate the extent of human debt to God, Jesus once told the story of a man who owed a king 10,000 talents (Matthew 18:22-35). A talent was a year's wage. Imagine being in debt equivalent to 10,000 years wages. But that's exactly how Jesus describes our condition before God.

On March 24, 1989, Captain Joe Hazelwood was sleeping below deck on the *Exxon Valdez* when it ran aground on a reef in Prince William Sound along the coast of Alaska. The resulting oil spill polluted 11,000 square miles of ocean and caked 1,300 miles of coastland with oil. Captain Hazelwood was found largely responsible for the spill. After years of litigation and clean up, the cost to Exxon approached $4 billion. Although Captain Hazelwood had been found largely responsible for the disaster, paying the debt of $4 billion was, of course, absurdly impossible for him.

Sins and trespasses put us into debt that far exceeds any capacity we can ever have to repay. To hate sin means to devote our lives to pure, noble, holy, and faithful living; we strive always to be in the places we should be; we resist at every turn going places we should not be; and in all things, we avoid accumulating a debt to God.

To sin is to do anything that lowers God's standard of living. And, of course, this reference is not to comfort and finance. God's standard of living is expressed as being:

…blameless and innocent, children of God without blemish in the midst of a crooked and perverse generation, in which you shine like stars in the world.
(Philippians 2:15)

When comedian W.C. Fields lay dying in his hospital bed, a friend was surprised to find him reading the Bible. He explained, "I'm checking for loopholes." The person who hates sin is not looking for loopholes and ways around the God-designed life. Instead, such a person is captured by what the Psalmist describes in this way:

Happy are those
who do not follow the advice of the wicked,
or take the path that sinners tread,
or sit in the seat of scoffers;
but their delight is in the law of the Lord,
and on his law they meditate day and night.
They are like trees
planted by streams of water,
which yield their fruit in its season,

and their leaves do not wither.
In all that they do, they prosper.
(Psalm 1:1-3)

Blessings flow through you into the world when you hate sin and resist it in every way.

Keep your heart with all vigilance,
for from it flow the springs of life.
(Proverbs 4:23)

Steve Stricker showed great promise as a young golfer, but for years, he was a disappointment on the professional tour—except for his character. Everyone agreed he was a good and decent man. And then, when he got into his forties, his game came around, and by 2008, he was one of the best golfers in the world. During one tournament where Stricker was doing particularly well, the head of the Professional Golfers' Association of America said about him, "If I had 150 golfers like Steve Stricker on the PGA tour, I could shut down the PGA office." It was his way of saying that people like Stricker do such a good job of managing themselves that they don't need management from others. Steve Stricker personifies justice.

Are you part of the world's management problem or part of its solution? Does your lifestyle mean your city needs more or fewer police officers, more or fewer auditors, more or fewer security personnel, more or fewer litter collectors, more or fewer marriage counselors, more or fewer janitors, more or fewer speed zones?

You bless the world by embracing Jesus as Lord and by doing justice and resisting evil in your daily life.

Bless justice by becoming a fountain of grace to sinners

Studying Jesus helps us see how a person who is wholly committed to a holy life responds to people trapped in bondage to sin. Jesus blessed people not only by hating sin, but also by making Himself an overflowing fountain of grace to sinners.

1. Give people time to think. When they brought the adulterous woman to Jesus in a rush to judge, Jesus pushed the pause button on the whole proceeding by kneeling down, writing on the ground with His finger, and saying absolutely nothing. He was opening up a little space for reflection.

Giving space and time for justice to work is the gracious thing to do because it gives time for our perspective to adjust. Jesus taught clearly on this when He said:

> *Do not judge, so that you may not be judged. For with the judgment you make you will be judged, and the measure you give will be the measure you get. Why do you see the speck in your neighbor's eye, but do not notice the log in your own eye? Or how can you say to your neighbor, "Let me take the speck out of your eye," while the log is in your own eye? You*

hypocrite, first take the log out of your own eye, and then you
will see clearly to take the speck out of your neighbor's eye.
(Matthew 7:1-5)

It's hard to do justice looking at things according to our own sinful nature. We need a new perspective. Each January and February, bald eagles migrate through Northern Idaho. They pause for a while in a bay along the Eastern shore of Lake Coeur d'Alene. Terri and I went one day to see the sight. Terri stood on a small ledge looking out over the lake and was enraptured by the sight of two majestic eagles perched on a nearby tree. I was just up the road and couldn't see what she saw. She kept giving me detailed instructions about the eagles' location, but hard as I tried, I couldn't see them. Finally she said, "Come stand by me," and when I did, there they were.

The person who is committed to the gracious exercise of judgment takes the time to stand where Jesus is standing, to see what Jesus sees.

2. Do not condemn. When these sinfully self-righteous men brought this sinful adulterous woman before the sinless man Jesus, He didn't condemn any of them. He didn't condemn the self-righteous men; He simply asked them to search out the condition of their own life. And He didn't condemn the woman; He simply told her to choose a better life, a pure and holy life.

We are told that the accusers went away one by one, beginning with the elders. The elders were the older, wiser, and more experienced members of the crowd. They were the ones others looked to. We don't know who the first was to walk away, but God bless him. If he hadn't walked away, who knows what might have happened. And God bless you if you walk away in similar situations. The power of ONE is never to be underestimated.

God does a better job of justice than we do. Our distorted vision warps perspective and causes us to act too quickly and to overreact. Like the family whose home was so overtaken by insects that they decided to solve the problem once-and-for-all. So they bought fifty insect foggers, scattered them through their 1,300 square foot house, closed the door and went to a movie. When they returned, they discovered the house had been blown off its foundation. It took $125,000 to repair the damage. Doing justice is a blessing to the world. Overdoing justice does damage to the world. Remember that only God knows how to do vengeance. Justice with skin on does all that it can to reflect the character of God. It also knows when to let go and leave the ultimate judgment to God.

As Paul wrote:

Beloved, never avenge yourselves, but leave room for the wrath of God; for it is written, "Vengeance is mine, I will repay," says the Lord.
(Romans 12:19)

Blessed to befriend humankind

In the end, only God knows how to apply the full extent of justice. Rather than being overcome by the need to "make things right" and to "correct every injustice," sometimes we are better off leaving the final resolution to God's greater wisdom. God will not be mocked, and in the end, He will make things right.

We bless others by doing justice Jesus' way, holding law and love together.

Tucked away in an off-the-beaten-track neighborhood in Taos, New Mexico, is a small cemetery. An iron entry gate identifies it as "The Cemetery of the Notables." Kit Carson is buried there along with other leaders from Taos' storied history. In a slightly overgrown side section is a gravestone bearing the name of *The Reverend F.F. Thomas — 1855-1921*. I looked and wondered what it took to gain entrance to "The Cemetery of the Notables." Then I noticed the brief inscription, "A friend of mankind." The one who is just—who lives according to God's beautiful design holding law and love together—is a friend of humankind. That's what makes a life notable. And the world longs for it. And the world is blessed by it.

DIALOGUE BOX

Your journal

When faced by injustice, what tends to motivate you to act? What tends to immobilize you?

Your prayers

Ask Jesus to bring to your mind a place where injustice is at work in your corner of the world.

Your discussion

- Jesus said He came to fill the law full of Himself. What happens when laws don't reflect the character of Jesus?

- Where do you tend to under-react or over-react to sinful behavior?

Your memory

Matthew 5:17-20

Your action

- Go to the courthouse and sit in on some trials and watch the judicial system in action. Write a one-page review of what you think it would be like to be on trial and what it would be like to be the judge.

PART FIVE

SERVE GENEROUSLY

Never think of yourself as anything other than a servant. As we have said, Jesus is the model human being, and He said of Himself:

> *...whoever wishes to become great among you must be your servant, and whoever wishes to be first among you must be slave of all. For the Son of Man came not to be served but to serve, and to give his life a ransom for many.*
> (Mark 10:43-5)

Generous service is the pulse that sets the rhythms of the universe.

But really? Never think of yourself as anything other than a servant? Wouldn't we rather *be* served than serve others—isn't that our natural wiring? The fitness center where I work out is surrounded by restaurants. I always arrive early in the morning, and the other day when I stepped out of my car, my foot found its way into the middle of someone's to-go box of leftover crawfish etouffee, dirty rice, and coleslaw.

The shrimp and rice oozed into the tread of my workout shoes. It was twenty feet from the trashcan, but someone apparently decided to leave his mess for someone else to clean up. Inside that fitness center is a line of sinks where men shave. Most men are pretty good about cleaning up after themselves, but some are slobs. In these sinks, some men leave great globs of shaving cream peppered with whiskers. It's gross! Who wants to use a sink full of someone else's whiskers?

You're probably thinking I should move to a better neighborhood, but from my experience, the neighborhood isn't the problem. The neighbors are. Jesus' life of self-giving service hardly appears to be most people's natural default setting. And here's the kicker. With the crawfish etouffee and rice pasted on my shoe, it only later occurred to me that I could have cleaned it up.

The flow of blessings

In the late 1800s, Chicago was a flourishing industrial center. At the time, the 156-mile Chicago River flowed through the city's neighborhoods and past its factories, collecting grotesque quantities of sewage and debris, eventually emptying into Lake Michigan—and polluting the city's drinking water. This problem was becoming a matter of life and death. The river was known as "the stinking river." But in 1900, in one of the great engineering feats of its day, using a series of locks, the flow of the river was actually reversed, allowing the fresh water from Lake Michigan to flow through the city, sweeping the river clean.

Jesus tells us that following Him requires a reverse of flow from being served to serving. For Jesus, serving others wasn't a hobby. It wasn't something He did on the side or when He had a spare minute or two. It was His chief occupation. But the problem with the life of service is that you give up the right to yourself—your time, your resources, your energy. The one thing most of us want is a life of our own. We crave the capacity to be in control. Relinquishing control, especially to the needs of the people around us, really goes against the grain.

After all, consider the work of the servant: To improve the quality of life for others. To relieve others' burdens. To increase their effectiveness. And these are the very things we want for ourselves. So who will take care of me?

In September 2002, Colin Pine was sitting at his work station in Denver doing contract translation work for the U.S. State Department. The phone rang and he found himself talking with Erik Zhang, cousin of the Houston Rockets basketball team's newest member, Yao Ming. The next thing Colin knew, he was Yao's full-time translator. He went everywhere with Yao – all the games, all the practices, all the press conferences, all team meetings. In fact, he moved into Yao's home and lived with his family. He put his own interests on hold. In one interview, he was asked what it was like being so tethered to another person. He answered, "His life is my life and that's fine with me."

My first response is to say, "Yes, but that's different." That's serving Yao Ming, NBA All Star, one of the most famous people in the largest country in the world. He played in front of multitudes. All of Colin's expenses are covered. He meets amazing people. Anyone would be happy to serve someone like Yao. I need to remember who I am serving.

Remember who you're serving

I need to remember who I am serving—Almighty God and His beloved people! No one gets more famous or important than that. We serve in front of the ranks and legions and multitude of the heavenly hosts. And in this service, God promises to supply every need according to His own unlimited resources.

To say, "His life is my life and that's fine with me" is the portal to a whole new realm of existence. It's a hard sell for God to convince us that this life of service is ultimately the most beautiful form of life, and Jesus doesn't want us to miss out on it.

Most people are familiar with the problem of passwords. I have to remember passwords for Amazon, my Apps store, my pension fund, my healthcare providers, various social networks, my bank, my computer at home, my computer at work, and on and on. It used to be a simple six- or eight-letter password was secure enough. But the requirements are getting more sophisticated because hackers can decipher simple passwords so easily. In fact, now they recommend twelve-character passwords instead of eight. It takes only an hour or two to break an eight-character password, but using even the most sophisticated software it takes 17,134 years to crack a twelve-character password. But the password to life's most beautiful form is still very simple. It is found in the five-letter code S-E-R-V-E.

It's true that the natural flow of the human mind is toward self—toward comfort, control, convenience, and consumption. The Bless Challenge involves reversing the natural flow of life from being served to serving others and to entering a realm of glorious meaning and purpose.

CHAPTER ONE

THE BLESSING:
Jesus Goes Slow and Works Small

Jesus tells us never to think of ourselves as anything other than a servant, and He's the model human being. So why are there so few who serve? One problem is that we can't see how it works. We can't predict the outcomes. So many variables and uncertainties exist. Will we be up to the challenge? And more importantly, who will take care of us? So we hold back. We settle for the amended life, the reduced life. Since we can't grasp the big-life that Jesus controls, we settle for the little-life that we control.

Hiking high in the Selkirk Mountains of Northern Idaho, the alpine trail to Hunt Lake passes through a massive boulder field. The boulders are the size of buses and small houses. The trail snakes its way through a shattered moonscape where no sign exists of hikers who have gone before you. It's easy to get disoriented and lost. So at strategic points, the Forest Service has sprayed large orange dots on certain boulders. You look for a dot on a distant boulder and figure out a way to get there, and then you look for the next dot. The way to Hunt Lake is a game of dot-to-dot.

Blessings awaiting

Serving Jesus is a game of dot-to-dot. He's gone before us to prepare the way. He leads us from point-of-service to point-of-service. After His resurrection when the disciples came looking for Jesus, they were told:

> ...he is going ahead of you to Galilee; there you will see him, just as he told you.
>
> (Mark 16:7)

Jesus is our pioneer. He goes before us. When it comes to serving others, we're not the pioneers—Jesus is. Service is not virgin, uncharted, or unexplored territory. Jesus has already been there. He intends to reassure us that we can approach the serving lifestyle, not with anxiety, but with anticipation.

> Let us run with perseverance the race that is set before us, looking to Jesus the pioneer and perfecter of our faith.
>
> (Hebrews 12:1-2)

The *pioneer* is the one who blesses by going before, preparing the way. Most human progress has been made possible by pioneers. Where would the world be without Christopher Columbus, Ferdinand Magellan, Lewis and Clark, Steve Jobs, Paul Allen, and Bill Gates?

Thomas Edison pioneered more than 1,000 inventions that have transformed the world. He predicted that he would make electricity so cheap that only the rich would use candles. The world was slow to catch on, so Edison illuminated one little street in New Jersey. When people saw this electrically-illuminated street, they made plans to illuminate their own streets. Edison was a pioneer.

Jesus is your pioneer. Every place you go, He's already illuminated the neighborhood, arranging things and getting things ready, painting dots on the rocks. Jesus prepares the way into every act of service—mercy, courage, generosity, justice, holiness, self-control, vision. Jesus doesn't simply have a life for you; He's already prepared the way into that life.

> *What no eye has seen, nor ear heard,*
> *nor the human heart conceived,*
> *what God has prepared for those who love him.*
> (1 Corinthians 2:9)

I once received a surprising invitation to be the guest conductor for the Mercury Baroque Orchestra's presentation of the Hallelujah Chorus during its Christmas presentation of Handel's *Messiah*. My first impulse was to run and hide. It's one thing to conduct an orchestra in the privacy of your car or shower, but to do so in front of an orchestra and a choir of professional musicians and a live audience was terrifying. But I found myself saying, "Yes," and only because it occurred to me that from time-to-time a person ought to do something that is entirely new. Even so, my palms started to sweat, and for weeks, I found myself staring at the ceiling in the middle of the night.

The artistic director, Antoine Plante, invited me to lunch to get acquainted. He handed me the score—a fat stack of papers with signs and marks and notes cascading down but meaning nothing to me. I bought the CD and played it over and over in my car while pretending to conduct. One time, I even rehearsed with the orchestra and chorus. And then it was show-time and I was on the stage in Jones Hall in downtown Houston. The artistic director had told me to relax because all they really needed me to do was to give some motion that gave the orchestra some reason to begin, and then four minutes and seven seconds later, to give some motion that suggested it was time to end, and they would take care of the rest. I found that bit of instruction both encouraging and deflating. And then I was on the stage...I don't have a clear recollection of what happened next. I think I reached to straighten my tie or scratch my ear and the orchestra took it as my sign to begin and out poured the music. The orchestra and choir rolled along, following notes and measures on pages, and at one point I found my-self thinking, "This is beautiful. I'm really good at this." But when I looked at the orchestra and surveyed the choir, I realized not one person was looking at me. And that's when I think I began to understand what it means that Jesus is our *pioneer.* The reason things were going so well with me up on that podium was because the artistic director had spent months in advance preparing the orchestra and choir for the presentation. The artistic director had been my *pioneer.*

When the Bible says:

> *We walk by faith and not by sight.*
> (1 Corinthians 5:7)

I think it means that Jesus has prepared things in advance in such a way that all we have to do is step forward with only a small measure of willing obedience and our act of faith will trigger amazing and wonderful developments all around us.

When it comes to service, just straighten your tie and the heavenly hosts will spring into action.

In his book, *The Ragamuffin Gospel,* Brennan Manning defines functional atheism as the belief that nothing is happening unless we are making it happen. The life of generous service doesn't make things happen; it reveals to us all the things that are already happening. It gets us in on the symphony that Jesus is already conducting all around us. Every conversation, every encounter, every obstacle, every event is a portal into an adventure that Jesus has already prepared.

CHAPTER TWO

THE APPLICATION:
Pioneer the Way for Others

The main challenge in serving is getting started. It's safe to say that most of us like the idea of serving others. We resonate with the general concept of service. We turn up the volume on heart-warming reports of service. We forward inspiring stories to our contact list. We even mull over possible forms of our own personal service. We think, we plan, we calculate—but the challenge comes with execution. Like the double-click on the computer mouse, there is often an enormous gap between the first click to select an action and the second click to execute.

When Elizabeth Thompson was fifty-seven years old, she was crippled by a stroke. She couldn't walk. Her physical therapy involved walking, swimming, and biking. After a year, she'd made a lot of progress. She didn't need the therapy anymore, but she didn't want to give up the discipline. That's when she heard about Iron Man competitions where contestants swim, bike, and run. So she trained and then she signed up—for the Iron Man Triathlon in Hawaii. A two-and-a-half-mile swim, followed by a 110-mile bike race followed by a 26.2-mile run. It took her seventeen hours of continuous effort but she made it to the end. Afterwards, a reporter commented on what a victory it was for her to cross the finish line. She responded, "For me the victory was crossing the STARTING LINE."

Say "YES" to blessing

Everything is a seed. Everything we own, every skill we have, every word we speak or thought we harbor is a seed with vast potential for expansion. The more broadly we broadcast, the more abundantly we harvest. We are deprived by what we keep for ourselves. The first step is to start—to plant—to invest—to go.

I inherited from my father a fascination with gardens. His soul seemed to flourish in the world of seeds and soils. I have a mental picture of him, hands on hips, dirty knees, muddy gloves, wearing worn-out wingtips. He was part of the generation that never dreamed of buying gardening clothes. He just waited for his dress clothes to wear out and then promoted them to their highest calling—yard work. He told me one time about a study done on the exponential potential in a watermelon seed. Breathtaking!

The point is this: the one who sows sparingly will also reap sparingly, and the one who sows bountifully will also reap bountifully.

(2 Corinthians 9:6)

But remember the big problem: even though service is the secret of life and it carries vast, exponential potential, it's not natural to us. It is not our first impulse. It takes half an hour or half a day or half a lifetime to decide to serve. We have to think it over, ponder it, consider its implications, ramifications, and obligations. It's our second thought, or our third, but not our first. Our natural tendency is toward self-interest.

In a city where I once lived, a fast food restaurant was just down the street from my office. Sometimes, I'd stop there for a meal. A girl worked there as a server. Sometimes she would take orders, and sometimes she'd pick up trays and wipe tables. And sometimes, right in the middle of her service, she'd shout, "NO!" Apparently, she suffered from some disorder that caused her involuntarily and spontaneously to blurt out the word "NO." When the word would explode from her mouth, it was a bit unsettling. She'd be wiping down a table or sweeping up a mess and suddenly shout, "NO!"

After a while, I began to wonder about the human tendency to respond to the need for service with an emphatic NO. That's the default position for human behavior. Accepting the BLESS Challenge changes the default position from NO to YES.

A child needs a mentor at school.

Turn NO to YES!

A widow needs repairs done to her home.

Turn NO to YES!

A neighbor falls and breaks a leg. Someone needs to mow the lawn.

Turn NO to YES!

It's the last week of a co-worker's employment. Someone needs to throw a party.

Turn NO to YES!

The church needs volunteers to work with children and youth.

Turn NO to YES!

Dogs get into the neighbor's garbage. Someone needs to clean up the mess.

Turn NO to YES!

The people who accept the BLESS Challenge to Serve Generously are those who learn to say YES.

Yes Man was a popular movie a few years back. In it, Jim Carrey played the part of Carl Allen, a bank employee whose negativism made him increasingly isolated and depressed. But then he attended a seminar on the power of "YES!" After the seminar, he took a vow to say, "Yes" to everything that came his way. His life was transformed. It was just a Hollywood story, but the truth in it is of biblical proportions.

For in Jesus every one of God's promises is a 'Yes.'
(2 Corinthians 1:18-20)

Something profound happens when we say, "YES!" Doors open, resources are released, the cosmos is stirred to cooperate. In the building where I work, several rooms have motion-activated lights. Sometimes, I try to outsmart them. I know I'm a grown-up and am supposed to be done with such silly things, but I can't resist. So I shift into ultra-slow-motion. But these sensors are so finely tuned I can't outsmart them, and even my smallest movement turns on the lights.

God is so turned on to acts of service that even the slightest move in that direction produces a light-filled response. Every time we say, "YES!" to God, God says, "YES!" in return. Just like with a seed. You bury the seed and a harvest will come.

The harvest of generous service is a blessing to the world.

DIALOGUE BOX

Your journal

If you knew that God would absolutely help you if you just started, what would you undertake to do to His glory?

Your prayers

Use Isaiah 41:10 as a guide to your prayer over the call to serve generously.

Your discussion

- How do you respond to the statement: *Never think of yourself as anything other than a servant?*

- Discuss the main "stoppers" to your attempts at generous service.

Your memory

Isaiah 43:18

Your action

- Make a list of your assets and time. Do you have enough, too much, or too little of each?

- Identify one short-term act of service you can do and follow through—preferably with a few other people.

CHAPTER THREE

THE BLESSING:
Jesus Perfects the Way for You

One time, Jesus told His disciples:

> *Be perfect, therefore, as your heavenly Father is perfect.*
> (Matthew 5:48)

That's not my favorite line in the Bible. Mostly because it seems impossible to be perfect when it is truly by our own effort. So it's important to remember that the Bible also says that Jesus is not only *the Pioneer* who goes before *preparing* the way, but He is also our *Perfecter* who comes along after perfecting our efforts, causing them to turn out far better than we could have made them on our own. Perfection is possible because of Jesus' service in us. Jesus helps us to finish well. As Paul said:

> *I am confident of this, that the one who began a good work among you will bring it to completion by the day of Jesus Christ.*
> (Philippians 1:6)

Jesus nudges us toward this *perfected* life in several ways.

The blessing of awakening purpose

By his own admission, Zacchaeus had been a thief and a cheat. His life was on a bad course. He had no sense of higher purpose. His life was destined to end poorly. But one day, Jesus walked into Zacchaeus's life, and by the time the day was over, Jesus had set Zacchaeus's life on a whole new track—a better track—a more perfect track (Luke 19:1-10). Zacchaeus went to bed that night a man reborn to noble purposes. We don't know what Jesus said or did beyond noticing Zacchaeus in the tree's branches and declaring His interest in spending the day with him, but we do know that Jesus' blessing set Zacchaeus on a course to finish his life well.

My parents came from what we would today call "dysfunctional" families. But they were determined not to pass this virus along to the next generation. My mother made her intentions clear in a letter she wrote to my dad a few weeks before their wedding. She wrote:

I can be extremely emphatic in saying that our children are going to love their home and look forward always to spending time there. I am educating myself, watching, listening, and reading about a desirable home so that from the very first moment our first child comes into the world our house is going to be to the children, God first, others second, and themselves last.

We're now three generations into my mother's vow and it continues to hold in her children, grandchildren, and great-grandchildren.

Jesus devoted His entire life to serving others. Every encounter He ever had caused people to recalibrate their destination to higher purpose and a better ending. His blessing changed the destinations of their lives.

The blessing of reconciling brokenness

Who doesn't want to finish well? A strong finish can make up for a poor start. And yet life funnels us down a thousand detours into brokenness.

Chris Wallace of the Arbinger Institute[1], tells a story of his father-in-law, who when he was fifteen years old, lived with his family in Southern Utah. Life for them was simple. The old Hudson wore out so they bought a new car, a 1952 Plymouth. One evening Chris' father-in-law asked his own father whether he could take the car into town. His dad lowered his glasses, put down his paper, thought for a moment and said, "Sure," and gave him the keys. He started down the lane and noticed the gas gauge read empty. He had no money so he backed up the car, went into the house and asked his dad for a few dollars. His dad lowered his glasses, put down his paper, and handed him some money. Back outside, the car was gone. Tracks through the dry grass

---

1 Taken from www.Arbinger.com, Accessed May 1, 2012.

led to the edge of the cliff along the Vernal River. Eighty feet down, there was the car, destroyed. He'd forgotten to set the parking brake. His head felt like it would explode. His stomach was turning inside out. What should he do? Back in the house, he explained to his dad about the parking brake and the cliff and the car. His dad lowered his glasses, put down his paper, thought for a moment, and said, "Then I guess you'll have to take the truck." And he went back to reading. About a quarter mile down the road, the boy had to pull over to the shoulder. He couldn't see through the tears. On the worst day of his life, his father had made things better. Think about what it must have been like for Peter on the worst day of his life. It must have been a crushing blow to deny Jesus so vigorously just before the crucifixion. It must have weighed on him heavily. At the worst possible moment, he turned from loyal friend to traitor. A few days after the resurrection, Jesus sought Peter out and gave him three opportunities to affirm his love for Him. That reconciliation set Peter on a new course and allowed Peter to finish his life and ministry in a more perfect way.

Chicago's O'Hare International Airport is named after World War II flying ace and Congressional Medal of Honor recipient, Butch O'Hare. He was credited with perhaps the most daring act of bravery in the history of combat aviation. Butch O'Hare was the son of Eddie O'Hare, the lawyer and business partner of mafia boss Al Capone. It has been reported that after Butch's birth, Eddie became increasingly uncomfortable with the life he was living and the legacy he was leaving for his son. And so, to give his son a better name, he offered himself as an informant against Al Capone. His testimony led to the downfall of Capone's empire of violence and corruption, and it also redeemed the O'Hare family name. The father served the son by setting the family on a different course.

Where you are is never so important as where you are headed. In Jesus' story of the Prodigal Son, as soon as the son turned around, the father ran to the far country to meet him. It wasn't a matter of location; it was direction that changed everything.

Jesus' plan for us is always to finish well. His service to humanity is to perfect us in the end. The hope we have in Jesus is that on the worst days of our lives, He makes things better.

The blessing of completed effort

There's a lot more going on in you and around you than you are making happen. As Paul said:

> *We know that all things work together for good for those who love God, who are called according to his purpose.*
> (Romans 8:28)

On a hillside, 5,000 people gathered around Jesus. It was late in the day and the Passover was coming. The disciples told Jesus to send the people home to eat. Jesus said, "You feed them." But they had no earthly idea how. A boy there had five barley loaves and two fish. In those days, a loaf of bread was the size of today's dinner roll and the word used here for *fish* designated fish the size of sardines. These words are carefully chosen to emphasize the contrast between what people have to offer and what Jesus can do with what they offer. They said, *What are they among so many people?* (John 6:9). Jesus had the people sit down on the grassy hillside, and, after giving thanks to God, He divided the bread and fish among the people until everyone had been *satisfied.* Then He had the disciples gather up the leftovers—twelve baskets full of leftovers. That meal had turned out far better than anyone dreamed possible.

I wonder what that boy was thinking when he offered his lunchbox to Jesus? I wonder what small fraction of that huge crowd he thought his loaves and fish would feed? He could never have imagined that Jesus would use so little food to feed so many people. But through our willingness, Jesus *perfects* our efforts; Jesus does more with what we offer, and He makes things turn out far better than we can imagine.

On January 15, 2009, US Airways flight 1549 took off from LaGuardia airport in New York on a routine flight to Charlotte. Within a minute, the flight became anything but ordinary. A flock of geese rendered both jet engines useless. Captain Sully Sullenberger weighed the three alternatives— try to glide back to LaGuardia, to glide to the airport in

Teterboro, New Jersey, or simply land in the Hudson River. Captain Sullenberger told air traffic control, "We'll be in the Hudson." He had to tell the disbelieving controller twice, "We'll be in the Hudson."

I think it's safe to say that when the engines quit on Flight 1549 that day, the main activity on board that aircraft was prayer. The passengers and crew were going to crash into the Hudson River. And everyone knows that a winged metallic cylinder weighing eighty-six tons that is aeronautically designed to fly at 31,000 feet is NOT designed to land and float like a cruise ship on the Hudson River. Yet beyond all expectations, that's what happened, and the photographs of 150 passengers and five crew members standing on the wings of the floating fuselage in the Hudson River will not soon be forgotten. I think it's safe to say that after a disastrous beginning, US Airways Flight 1549 turned out far better than anyone could have expected. Somehow, Captain Sullenberger's efforts had been perfected!

Eventually, the airplane was hauled out of the Hudson River and a museum was built for it in Charlotte. I wish I could have moved it in our parking lot here in Houston. I'd put up ladders for people to climb to stand on the wing and to remember that Jesus has ways to make things turn out far better than we can imagine. It could be a kind of holy place where frightened, desperate, hopeless people could gather and remember how God promises:

For He will command his angels concerning you
to guard you in all your ways.
On their wings they will bear you up,
so that you will not dash your foot against a stone.
You will tread on the lion and the adder,
the young lion and the serpent you will trample under foot.
Those who love me, I will deliver;
I will protect those who know my name.
When they call to me, I will answer them;
I will be with them in trouble,
I will rescue them and honour them.
With long life I will satisfy them,
and show them my salvation.
(Psalm 91:11-16)

Jesus is our Perfecter. For reasons we can't explain, life turns out better than we have any right to expect. Our marriage, our children, our work, our service—they all turn out better—when we trust Him.

Jesus finds ways to serve that help people's lives turn out for the better. What a gift. It's so perfect.

When it comes to serving generously, all we have to do is to start. The first step in serving is the victory step. After that, Jesus pioneers and *perfects* our efforts.

CHAPTER FOUR

THE APPLICATION:
Perfect the Way for Others

You bless others by doing all you can to help their lives turn out well. Ravi Zacarias described touring a Sari factory in India. One section of the factory was used for weaving the fabrics. These fabrics are among the most beautiful and delicate in all the world. The looms for weaving the fabrics were simple. A man worked from an upper platform. He chose the colors and threads and design. Another man worked from a lower platform. He simply moved the shuttle back and forth. In most cases, they were father-and-son teams. The son didn't really have an idea what the father was doing until he moved the shuttle across the loom. Then, slowly the pattern took shape.

You bless others by helping them keep their shuttle moving. By keeping moving, you help God's beautiful pattern in their lives to emerge. After all, life can be discouraging. Progress can be slow. We can lack mental models for what can be. We can become immobilized or distracted.

In 2008, Rick Kell was working at Walter Reed Army Hospital. He kept hearing the same story from soldiers who had been seriously wounded in the war in Iraq. "I wanna go back." At first, this desire didn't make any sense to Rick. Why would they want to go back to the place where they'd suffered such crippling injuries and nearly been killed? Gradually, it became clear that they wanted to go back because they'd never left. After their injuries they were airlifted out of Iraq, often in a coma, and awakened in the hospital. It seems that from the day a soldier arrives in Iraq, that soldier begins to think about the day he will leave. What will he have for his last meal, how will he celebrate, what will it be like to pack the duffle bag for the last time? Soldiers imagine boarding the air transport, watching the ground fall away, arriving to a joyful homecoming. But for them, those things never happened. They never really came back. So Rick Kell came up with the idea of Operation Proper Exit. He takes these wounded warriors back to Iraq, to the place they were wounded, and to the triage center where they were first treated. They get to see the place, to thank the medical personnel, to board the transport, to watch the ground fall away, to arrive to a homecoming celebration. Rick Kell blesses these wounded soldiers by getting them back on the right track.[1]

We all live lives interrupted by brokenness. What a blessing it is to be put back on the right track.

---

1 *60 Minutes*. November 6, 2011.

The blessing of awakening purpose

There's no guarantee that a good start will produce a good finish, but at the very least, it's true that it's hard to overcome a bad start. It is widely known that the first three years of a child's life are critical in every way. A lot of attention is also given to what's called the *4-14 Window*, the period of time between the ages of four and fourteen when, for 85 percent of people, the deepest convictions about God, purpose, and place in the universe are established. If this *4-14 Window* closes without these convictions being formed, then a person tends to become a spiritual drifter. One of the greatest forms of service we can offer is to help children establish their spiritual identity.

Manfred Honeck is the music director of the Pittsburgh Symphony Orchestra. Honeck's decision to become a musician and conductor came about in an instructive way. As a boy, he went one year with his father to the New Year's Eve concert at the Vienna Philharmonic. It's a famous and enormously popular concert. The crowd was so large that Honeck couldn't get anywhere near the orchestra. But a kindly usher noticed him and brought him to the front. "I got the fire for being a conductor, or professional musician," he said. "If this usher did not put me in this position, I would not have done this."[2] Today, Honeck is well-known for his deep Christian faith. He has built a chapel in his

2 *New York Times.* February 19, 2010.

home where he regularly worships. He routinely meets and prays with musicians before concerts.

I can't imagine that usher had any idea how his simple act of service would establish a child's place in the universe. Every child—every person—needs an usher. We join Jesus in His serving ministry when we look out for children, on the one hand protecting them from danger and the ugliness of life, and on the other, exposing them to the myriad forms of service that following Jesus can afford.

Think of yourself as an usher at the concert of life, giving the people around you of all ages a front-row seat to the glorious purposes of God.

The blessing of reconciling brokenness

It is said that when King David came to the end of his life, he lay down in his bed and was *satisfied.* If you are familiar with David's life, you know it was a porridge of glory and horror. Each of his victorious accomplishments was offset by brutish disobedience. And yet at the end, he was satisfied—he finished well.

Who wants to finish poorly? You may know the story of Chuck Colson, Special Counsel to President Richard Nixon and one of the Watergate Seven. As a result of the Watergate scandal, Chuck Colson fell from glory to shame and spent seven months in a federal prison after pleading guilty to obstruction of justice. But at the low point of his life, he met

Doug Coe, leader of The Fellowship and according to *TIME Magazine*, one of the twenty-five most influential people in Washington, D.C. He's influential, not because of his politics or high profile, but because of his faith. Doug Coe works under the radar. When Chuck Colson needed a friend, Doug Coe befriended him and introduced him to Jesus Christ. After his seven months in prison, Colson founded the Prison Fellowship and the Chuck Colson Center for Christian Worldview. He was awarded the Templeton Prize of more $1 million for having made "exceptional contributions to affirming life's spiritual dimension." He donated the prize to the Prison Fellowship.

Every person has a broken place in his or her life. And in everyone there is a deep longing for healing. An editorial in *The Boston Globe* from 1973 speaks for all of us, "If Mr. Colson can repent of his sins there just has to be hope for everybody. But this act of repentance is almost always fueled by a person like Doug Coe."

It helps to think of Jacob. He was the second-born son of Isaac. For whatever reasons, he was a thief and a scoundrel who deceived his father and stole from his brother. His life was a long journey of from-bad-to-worse. Once, Jacob wrestled with God, and God gave him a limp. Along the way, Jacob's brother, Esau, came looking for him. Jacob assumed the worst, but when his brother found him, he ran to him, embraced him, and wept with joy over him. Esau's greeting was so unexpected. It was so out-of-proportion to all of Jacob's deception. At that moment of reconciliation, Jacob stammered:

> *Truly to see your face is like seeing the face of God—since you have received me with such favor.*
> (Genesis 33:10)

Everyone needs an Esau—someone who offers the service of reconciliation and restoration. Every person leaves a lot of debris in life. The major hurdle to ending well—to a perfected life—is restoration of broken relationships.

Someone in your life needs you to be Esau and to offer a service of reconciliation that is out of proportion to the brokenness. What greater blessing can there be than this blessing?

The blessing of completion

I once had a conversation with the legendary and ageless entertainer, Pat Boone. He told me that he couldn't imagine "retiring." His mind bristled with ideas. After a pause, he said, "My wife, Shirley, tells me I am an 'A-and-Z' man. I can see the beginning of a project, and I can see the end. I just can't see any of the letters in between so I have a hard time finishing what I start."

When I heard Boone say that, I felt an electrical jolt because he was describing me. I get ideas. I can see how things need to be. But I tend not to have any good ideas to get from A to Z. When I told my realization to my wife, Terri, she said, "That's so interesting because I'm just the opposite. I have no visionary ideas. But if someone comes up with A and Z, I can figure out the letters from B and C to X and Y."

Thomas Friedman, *New York Times* columnist, was once asked, "What's your favorite form of renewable energy?" He answered, "It's 10,000 people in 10,000 garages." So many great ideas are simmering in so many garages. When it comes to putting life together, no one has all the letters of the alphabet, but everyone has a few.

I have started projects and gotten stuck at letter B. I can testify to the blessing of a servant arriving with the next letter—the B or H or L or Q, and offering, "Can I help you with that?"

Sometimes, we get stuck because we run out of ideas. Sometimes, we get stuck because life gets in the way. Sometimes, we get stuck because the vision is bigger than we can manage.

I don't know what kind of name to give to this kind of service; maybe it's the quiet service of alphabet soup. Whatever it is, you are surrounded by people who are stuck in the middle of something and they don't know how to move forward, but you have a letter you can offer to fill in the alphabet of their efforts, and if you offer it, it will be a beautiful blessing.

Years ago, I read a news report of the theft of Tammy Rogers' 1972 Mazda. It was sometime in the mid-1980s, and the car was in such bad shape that not a single part of it wasn't dented, cracked, rusted, or broken. It wasn't worth much, but nonetheless, she filed a police report. Nine months later, the police called to say her car had been recovered. She went to the impound lot and looked at the collection of automobiles, but none was her '72 Mazda. There was a '72 Mazda in one of the spaces, but it was clearly not hers. It was in mint condition. When she asked, "Where's my car?" they pointed to the perfect Mazda. "But it's not mine; it's perfect," she said. The police insisted, "Yes, it's yours; the serial number matches." Apparently, the thieves who had stolen the car had completely restored it. It had been *perfected.*

Jesus' service of blessing to us is that He *perfects* us. He takes our broken-down efforts, our dented, cracked, rusted, broken-down lives, and He restores them. He restores us to the glory of our original serial number.

Bob Pierce, founder of World Vision, said, "Don't fail to do something just because you can't do everything" (Stearns 152). Don't ever underestimate the power of small things. Remember that old Chinese proverb, "The longest journey begins with a single step." Anne Lamott, in her book, *Bird by Bird*, says that the key to writing a book is to write a really awful first draft. Just starting is 90 percent of the work. I have heard it said that when launching a rocket into deep space, 90 percent of the fuel is used in the first few minutes. Just getting started is most of the battle. And having someone push or pull or clear the way makes all the difference.

An old story tells of a king who sponsored a race for all the men of his realm. The prize was a sack of gold coins. The king determined not to award the prize until the last runner crossed the finish line. After a long delay, finally, the last runner struggled home. The man was cut and bruised and apologized for his delay. He explained that on the course he had encountered a large pile of stones and debris. He had been concerned for his fellow runners so he stopped and moved the debris off the course. The stones were large and many were sharp, so he wounded himself as he worked. That's when the king surprised everyone by announcing that this last runner was in fact the victor. As he awarded the gold coins to the runner, the king said, "He runs best who makes the way easier for those who follow."

Jesus blesses us as the pioneer who goes before us and the perfecter who comes after us. We, as His agents who have been sent by Him to continue His mission, are pioneers and perfecters for those around us.

Isn't it strange, that princes and kings,
and clowns that caper in sawdust rings,
and common-folk like you and me,
are builders for eternity?

To each is given a bag of tools,
a shapeless mass and a Book of Rules;
and each must make 'ere time has flown,
a stumbling block or a stepping stone.

— R.L. Sharpe, *A Bag of Tools*, circa 1809

DIALOGUE BOX

Your journal

When you think over your life, where do you have regret that you didn't follow through more completely?

Your prayers

Ask God to remind you of the areas of unfinished
business in your life.

Your discussion

- Do you find yourself to be a better starter or
  finisher?

- Which people in your life have made the difference
  between finishing poorly and finishing well?

Your memory

Philippians 1:6

Your action

- Recommit yourself to finishing a project you
  started.

- Find a person who seems stuck in the middle of a
  project he can't finish without help and volunteer
  to help him finish well.

CHAPTER FIVE

THE BLESSING:
God Will Supply Your Every Need

Fear of not having enough must be one of the most fundamental human anxieties. It is so deep in our DNA that one of a child's first words is usually "More." I was raised in strict simplicity. My parents recycled before the word "recycle" existed. My dad bought powdered milk in large tubs and my mom mixed it with water and put it in empty mayonnaise jars. I remember the first time I saw mayonnaise jars in the store and wondered why they put mayonnaise in milk jars. We saved the tinsel from the Christmas tree and ironed it. We ate a lot of spam and beef tongue. My mother would go to the U-Pick fields, pick vegetables, and bring them home to can. I think her motto was: "Why have it fresh if you can have it canned?" My mom took care of the books every Sunday afternoon. She sat at her little desk in the living room, balancing the accounts to the penny. It usually left her depressed because we could never seem to get ahead. I remember how she'd say, "We don't have any problems that another five dollars wouldn't solve." It's the sort of thing you'd expect someone to say who was living just down the street from the poverty line. That's why it's odd but also instructive to remember what John D. Rockefeller, at the time one of the richest men in the world, replied when he was asked the question, "How much is enough?" He answered, "Just a little more."

Apparently "enough" does not exist and it bears little relationship to what you've got. In their book *Switch: How to Change Things When Change is Hard,* Chip and Dan Heath describe an experiment that was conducted using popcorn. Moviegoers were given popcorn in very large containers—some were larger than others, but each container was huge—far more than any human could possibly consume. Now the catch was the popcorn was really, really, really old—popped days before and left out to get ridiculously stale, so stale it squeaked on your teeth. When the movie was over, the amount of popcorn eaten was measured, and it was discovered that the larger the container, the more the people ate. It appears that human beings can never get enough! No matter how much we've got, we want more! Life is driven by the fear of lack!

The fear spills over into our relationship with God. A few days after the Chilean mine collapse in the summer of 2010, relief workers drilled a three-inch diameter shaft through 2,500 feet of rock to reach them. For the next seventy days until their rescue, everything those miners received from above had to fit through a three-inch pipe. I went to the hardware store and bought a section of that pipe so I could see what it looked like. It's small. Not much fits through a supply line that small. We often worry that God supplies us that way—through something like a three-inch pipe. How can we possibly get "enough" when the supply comes through a tight three-inch pipe.

Here is where the big surprise comes. Pay close attention to what the Bible announces:

> *And God is able to provide you with every blessing in abundance, so that by always having enough of everything, you may share abundantly in every good work.*
>
> (2 Corinthians 9:8)

God is able to provide you with every blessing

Always having enough of everything... God is not a three-inch provider.

First, understand that you are not the originator. You are not in *supply*; you are in *delivery*. The only miracle told in all four gospels concerned the feeding of the multitude. A large crowd gathered to listen to Jesus. Reports said four or five thousand, not counting women and children. The major holiday of Passover was near. It was late. The stores would be closing. The disciples grew concerned for the welfare of the large crowds and told Jesus to send the people home. Jesus turned to Philip and told him, *You give them something to eat.* It may have been because Philip was from that region and would have known where the supermarkets were. He did some mental calculations based on the crowd estimate and the amount each person would eat. He developed a formula and determined, *Even eight months wages wouldn't be enough to give each one a little.* Because he thought the burden of supply was on him, he concluded that the situation was, in a word, hopeless!

While Philip was making his mental calculations, Andrew decided to do an inventory of the local resources, and he came back with the similarly discouraging report of only five dinner rolls and two sardines. There may have been more but that's as much as anyone was willing to give. His conclusion was the same. The situation was hopeless.

The disciples were under the mistaken impression that they were the originators of the supply when what Jesus really expected of them was to be deliverers of what He would supply. Jesus never asked Philip to run the numbers on cost. He never asked Andrew to calculate the available resources in the crowd.

If we wait to begin service until we have *enough*—time, money, energy—we'll never get started. But the Bible's driving message is this: *God is able!*

Blessings in abundance

From what I can tell from scripture and experience, the only thing that restricts God's supply is my generosity. The more

I trust and act, the more God moves through me. God is not a God of poverty but of abundance. There's never any sense that God worries about balancing the books or coming up short. There's no threat that God may need to file for bankruptcy or petition for a bailout.

I rented a car in California not long after the state's new environmentally sensitive gas pumps had been installed. These pumps were designed to shut off the flow at the slightest hint of a leakage. When I went to refill the gas tank before returning the rental car, I couldn't seem to get more than three-cents worth of gas down the fill spout before the pump would click off and I'd have to reset. Do you have any idea how long it takes to fill a fifteen-gallon tank three-cents worth at a time with gas at $3.50 a gallon—that's 116 interruptions—116 resets per gallon. The supply comes, but very slowly.

But God is not a three-cent at a time provider. God provides in abundance. Former President Jimmy Carter said, "My faith demands—this is not optional—my faith demands that I do whatever I can, wherever I am, whenever I can, for as long as I can with whatever I have to try and make a difference." That attitude opens the pipeline and taps into the limitless wealth of God's supply.

One time, our church gave out $20,000 to our members. We divided the money into 600 envelopes that ranged in amounts from $6 to $1,000. We told the people to go bless someone with the money. It was like sending out 600 missionaries. Betty Irwin found $10 in her envelope and wondered what to do. Then it occurred to Betty that she liked making dinner rolls from scratch. So she used her $10 to buy ingredients, made a few batches of rolls, and went to her friends and said, "I'd like to give you some rolls, but they aren't free. You need to make a donation to Living Water International." At last count, Betty's $10 had passed $1,000. And that's what I'm talking about. That's what I mean when I say that we do not have a three-inch, three-penny God. He owns the universe and invites you to join Him in creating things the way He does—as a servant.

As Paul went on to say:

> *...so that by always having enough of everything, you may share abundantly in every good work.*
> (2 Corinthians 9:8)

We have what we have in order to bless others with abundance. What you have is your tool, and God desires that you do something BIGGER with it.

ABC News once honored Jim Mayer as its Person of the Week. At the age of twenty-three, Mayer had gone off to Vietnam with a brand new business degree from his college and a rifle from the U.S. Army. He stepped on a landmine. It blew him straight up in the air. He knew that his injuries were bad (he lost both legs). On the way down, he said to himself, "I am going to live. So it's kind of like: Okay, this is bad. This is not good. But I'm going to live. I became determined immediately to get over it." He went to work for the Department of Veterans Affairs, and in 1991, during the Persian Gulf War, he began visiting amputees in Ward 57 of Walter Reed Medical Center in Washington, D.C. He arrived there every week with his two titanium legs and arms full of milkshakes. He used the milkshakes as an icebreaker and a conversation starter to get to deeper things. No one knew about his legs until later when he showed them. Then they were all amazed. The wounded warriors called him The Milkshake Man. Mayer is an example of one who doesn't let what he doesn't have stop him from making more of what he does have. He's discovered that you can do a lot with the little you've got left in life.

Serving generously exposes that we do not have a three-inch, three-cent God. Our God is one who blesses us with everything in abundance in order that we might bless others through generous service.

CHAPTER SIX

THE APPLICATION:
Give as You've Made Up Your Mind

As I mentioned earlier, people think somewhere between 12,000 and 30,000 thoughts a day. A bridge in Austin, Texas is famous for being home to a vast colony of bats. At dusk, the bats swarm out in great clouds. Sometimes, my mind feels like that—like a colony of bats that flock off in all directions. These thoughts carry us from the lofty to the lowly, from the noble to the grotesque. Most of us would be embarrassed for people to know the thoughts we think. Service that blesses requires disciplining the thought-patterns of the mind.

The mind that blesses

To discipline our mind to be one that blesses, three mental shifts are necessary:

1. Train your mind to recognize need. Because generous service is not our first nature, our minds are not even programmed to recognize the need for service. Like learning to write with the other hand, it takes practice. Develop sensitivity to people in need, an instinct to improve a situation, an awareness of brokenness, and a deep conviction that serving generously is not your secondary activity but your primary activity! Service is the very reason you are where you are.

Recently, I had a lunch appointment and wanted to remind myself of the restaurant's location. I went to its website and found the Google Earth locator. Just then, I noticed a box in the corner that asked, "Do you want to save this location?" And suddenly, I imagined God Googling earth and seeing the box with that question, "Do you want to save this location?" and pausing for a moment before checking the box, "Yes!"

> *For God so loved the world that He sent His only Son,*
> *that whoever believes in Him might not perish but have*
> *everlasting life.*
> (John 3:16)

The Bible goes on to teach us to:

> *Let the same mind be in you that was in Christ Jesus...*
> (Philippians 2:5)

Generous service requires shifting the mind to want to join God in His life-saving, earth-saving activity. God's desire is that we should think His thoughts, and that begins by recognizing need.

Some people brought to Jesus a blind man. Jesus laid His hands on him and asked, "Can you see anything? The man squinted and answered, I can see people, but they look like trees, walking." So Jesus laid His hands on him a second time and his sight was restored and he saw everything clearly (Mark 8:22-25).

I am that man. I need a second touch to see people. We don't actually see with our eyes. Our eyes are merely the receptors of images. We really see with our mind. The mind receives the image and interprets what it sees. It is the mind that learns to "see" the need and respond.

For me, this seeing requires a supernatural intervention. I have perfected such a finely developed avoidance system that I don't even see need when it stares me right in the face. I am very much like the cartoon character, Mr. Magoo, who blindly bumbles through life without ever noticing all the chaos around him. So I pray for supernatural awakening to need—to see people, not as *trees walking*, not as objects to be avoided, but as people, as God's own beloved, awaiting a blessed embrace.

2. Discipline your mind to act on second and third-thought. Don't be surprised to discover that even after you begin to notice a need for service, serving generously still won't be your first impulse or even your second or your third. You will often be down the street, around the corner, and in your car before your mind finally convinces you to go back. Turning around and going back is an important discipline of the will.

For my part, service is rarely my first thought, so I've tried to change the natural flow of my mind through the practice of picking up trash. Whenever I see trash, I try to see it as a chance to serve. The problem, of course, is that trash is trashy! It's dirty and inconvenient. The filthiest trash usually crosses my path right after I've washed my hands. I have developed a suspicion that God sends trash my way at strategic moments when I'm in a hurry going somewhere else. So it usually takes a block or two for me finally to respond. This practice has taught me a simple lesson. Once you see something, you can't un-see it. Once you know something, you can't un-know it. The need for service is evident all around us. The BLESS Challenge pushes us to recognize and then to respond to what we see and know.

Kevin Ford told me about a man named Rick Hurst who travelled a great deal, and because of budget limitations, he always stayed in cheap motels. One time, however, he stayed at the Ritz Carlton. His lavish room included sitting, sleeping, and dressing areas, and several sinks along with a tub and shower. Each sink, tub, and shower had its own supply of soap, and not like the slivers of soap you find in cheap motels. These were big, fat bars of soap. And they were the best soaps he'd ever used. So he did what lots of people do; he gathered them up and put them in his suitcase. Every day after the maid serviced the room, he'd gather up the soaps. One day, he came in and found his bed, ringed like a halo, with big, fat bars of Ritz Carlton soaps. And in the middle of the bed, a note:

> Dear Mr. Hurst. We're glad you like our soaps. Please take these, and if you'd like more, just let us know.

I wonder how many days it took for the maid to recognize this unique opportunity to bless. Discipline your mind to be on the lookout for ways to bless, even on second and third-thought.

3. Learn to counter mental objections. After a lifetime of practice, your mind is deeply committed to its own comfort. And control. Every need for service will be countered with a mental chorus of "I can't!" "Not now!" "Let someone else!" Your mind will even try to convince you that it didn't notice the need to serve. Your mind will try to convince you not to jump in.

My dad didn't learn to swim until he was grown. It was my mom who drove him to it. She loved to swim and to vacation on water, so my dad decided he'd better face his fear. Off he went to the YMCA. His first day was terrifying. And they didn't start at the shallow end. Down at the deep end, they gave simple instructions, "Jump in, put your arms out, your head back, relax, and watch what happens." Years later, he described it in quiet, reverent tones. First the terror of the deep and the cold suffocating water closing over his head, all familiar sounds suddenly muffled in fluid. And then, with his heart exploding, he felt something like hands come up beneath him, gently lifting him to the surface and suspending him safely in the water. He claimed to have learned more theology in that moment than in three years of seminary—how when we act in faith, God responds.

For he will command his angels concerning you
to guard you in all your ways.
On their hands they will bear you up,
so that you will not dash your foot against a stone.
(Psalm 91:11-12)

As the old saying goes, "Swimming is a lot more interesting at the deep end of the pool." Life is no different. It gets more interesting when we jump in over our head and serve.

The battle of the mind is fought on many fronts. Some are minor skirmishes; some are more like the Normandy Invasion. But generous service begins in this way:

Each of you must give as you've made up your mind.
(2 Corinthians 9:7)

When Bill Strong retired, he wondered what to do with his life. He'd always had an interest in books so he began volunteering at the Princeton Public Library—repairing books, mostly children's books. At last count, he had repaired more than 3,000. One of Bill Strong's favorite memories is of a grandfather who brought to him a worn-out book that his grandfather had inscribed and given to him when he was a boy. Now a grandfather himself, he wanted to repair the book so he could inscribe it, fly to Denver, and give it to his grandson. Above the desk of Strong's workshop at home he keeps a small postcard that reads:

The hands

those precious, wonder instruments

ask for some creative occupation.

The power of blessing is released when through generous service we begin to say, "Yes" to God's creative occupation!

And when the moment comes that you think you can't, remember the old African saying:

If you think you are too small to make a difference, try spending the night in a closed room with a mosquito.[1]

God designed you to be a difference maker, and His chief tool in your hands is the power of blessings.

---

1 Quoted in *A Hole in Our Gospel* by Richard Stearns

DIALOGUE BOX

Your journal

So now that you've dipped your toe into the waters of generous service, what have you learned about yourself and about God?

Your prayers

Confess the fears you have over serving generously.

Your discussion

- In what ways have you protected yourself from recognizing the need for service in the world?

- Confess the places you tend to "stockpile" out of fear that you won't have enough.

Your memory

Philippians 4:19

Your action

- Choose an area of chronic human need and begin to make yourself more familiar with the issues involved.

- Write out a certificate of surrender whereby you commit yourself to a life of generous service and have it "notarized" by your group members or a friend.

THE BLESS CHALLENGE

How long has it been since God restarted history by announcing to Abraham:

I will bless you, and make your name great, so that you will be a blessing. I will bless those who bless you, and...in you all the families of the earth shall be blessed.

(Genesis 12:2-3)

Historical estimates suggest it's been about 4,000 years. Most of us have a hard time remembering what we had for breakfast, let alone something that happened in ages and epochs before we were born.

Blessing! It is God's brilliant strategy for turning our lives, history, and world around. In these pages, my hope has been to restore our memory to the power of blessings.

As we have seen in these pages, the act of blessings requires, first of all, a discipline of the will. You may have heard of the ranch in Montana where they broke wild horses. It was a job mostly done by tough and experienced cowboys who knew how to stay on the horse until it was submissive to the will of its rider. But every once in awhile, a horse would come along that was too wild for even the most experienced cowboy to tame. So, in those cases, an old mule would be tied to the wild horse and the two would be let free to go across the plains together. The wild horse didn't like being attached to anyone, so off it went in a cloud of dust and a flurry of flying hooves. But after a few days, they'd return, and in returning, while the mule was bruised and bloodied, the wild horse was tame.

The discipline of blessing others requires us to stay connected to people even when their hooves are flying and their clouds of dust make us choke. It requires us to hold on even when we bear in our own bodies the cuts and bruises that others inflict upon us.

And secondly, the act of blessing requires a setting of the heart. For 4,000 years, God has been working the BLESS Challenge. I often wonder how He keeps at it. Aren't their limits to His patience and goodwill? How can God do this FOREVER? I was in the grocery store with Terri the other day. She was thumbing over the avocados while I was minding the grocery cart. It was about as simple and ordinary a moment as there can be in life. As I stood there, the thought rolled through my mind, "I could do this forever." You can do forever only what you love. God's plan to transform history and humanity through the power of blessings is driven by His inexhaustible love. Not by sheer gritty determination, but because it gives God pleasure to stay in the game with us. The deep truth is that God finds pleasure in stacking up blessings on people who don't deserve them. A few years ago, John Piper got interested in the things that give God pleasure and wrote a remarkable book, *The Pleasures of God: Meditations on God's Delight in Being God.* Piper explored every reference to *the pleasure of God.* Passages like:

> *Do not be afraid, little flock, for it is your Father's*
> *good pleasure to give you the kingdom.*
> (Luke 12:32)

The setting of the heart is essential. My son Grant and I were fishing on a river in Colorado. He's an excellent fisherman and I'm just a hacker. He had all the gear and I just wore sneakers and shorts. At one point along the river, one section was separated from the other by a high cliff. To get from one section to the other, you followed a trail up one side and down the other. In the middle of the day, I took that hike. At the top, I stopped for the view. In the wide pool below stood my son working his fly line on the four-point arc between 10 a.m. and 2 p.m. It was artistry in motion. As I looked down, I thought how much I loved him and how proud I was of him. Later in the day, I told him that. He replied, "That's interesting, Dad, because the same thing happened to me when I was climbing that trail and saw you fishing below." The BLESS Challenge is fueled by sharing in God's deep pleasure in looking in on history.

The 2010 Governor's race in Texas included the usual sloganeering by the candidates. Back and forth the ads jostled, "He's in it for Texas" or "He's in it for himself." After enduring the usual onslaught of political advertising, this tag line eventually got buried in my mind in such a way that as I wrote in my journal early one morning, God seemed to ask that very question of me. "Who are you in it for, Dave? Are you in it for yourself or for Me?" It didn't take a blink of an eye for me to know that most of the time and on most occasions, I'm in it for me. That's the central symptom of the human problem. But since coming to know Jesus, there is another part of me that's not like that. There's another part of me that wants to be in it for my faithful Savior, Jesus Christ, who at the price of His own life, has given my life back to me.

Yard work has always been my main recreational pleasure. Weeds, fungus, and disease have always been the chief enemy of this pleasure. When we lived in Eastern Washington, we had a large yard with lots of grass and the grass was home to necrotic ring spot disease. It's a fungus that produces donut or frog's-eye shaped patches of dead lawn. Despite years of research and experimentation, it remains one of the more pesky agricultural problems. I tried all the home remedies and paid for chemical treatments, but always the spots would reappear, then it was suggested that I try over-seeding the lawn. This process simply involved using an aerator machine to punch thousands of finger-sized holes in the lawn, scattering ring spot resistant ryegrass seed over the lawn, and raking the seeds into the holes. What followed was a miracle. The seeds filled in the dead patches and resisted the advancement of the fungus. My lawn turned green again.

Take this principle of over-seeding out of the yard and into the landscape of your life. When God told Abraham He would bless him to be a blessing, He was telling him to become an over-seeder, one who sowed life into death, and light into darkness, and hope into despair. For Abraham, for you and for me, the challenge is to receive God's blessings and then to sow them into others' lives and to change the world one blessing at a time.

DIALOGUE BOX

Your journal

How has your awareness of the power of blessings been impacted by this experiment in receiving and giving God's blessings?

Your prayers

Pray that The BLESS Challenge will become your way of life. Develop a pattern for beginning each day with a prayer to bless others.

Your discussion

- What has it been like for you to be an agent of blessing in new situations?

- How has this affected your sense of purposeful living?

Your memory

1 Chronicles 4:10

Your action

- Write a one-page covenant for receiving and passing God's blessings to others.

WORKS CITED

BOOKS:

Arbinger Institute. *Leadership and Self-Deception: Getting Out of the Box*. San Francisco, CA: Berrett-Koehler, 2010.

Baillie, John. *A Diary of Readings*. New York, NY: Charles Scribner's Sons, 1955.

Bell, Rob. *Velvet Elvis: Repainting the Christian Faith*. Grand Rapids, MI: Zondervan, 2005

Bible. New Revised Standard Version. Nashville, TN: World Publishing, 1997.

Brand, Paul and Philip Yancey. *Fearfully and Wonderfully Made: A Surgeon Looks at the Human and Spiritual Body*. Grand Rapids, MI: Zondervan, 1980.

Bryson, Bill. *A Short History of Nearly Everything*. Portland, OR: Broadway Books, 2003.

Dillard, Annie. *Pilgrim at Tinker Creek*. New York, NY: HarperCollins, 1974.

Foer, Joshua. *Moonwalking with Einstein: The Art and Science of Remembering Everything.* London, Gr. Brit.: Penguin, 2011.

Gladwell, Malcolm. *Outliers: The Story of Success.* New York, NY: Little, Brown and Company, 2008.

Hawking, Stephen and Leonard Mlodinow. *The Grand Design.* New York, NY: Bantam Books, 2010.

Heath, Chip and Dan Heath. *Switch: How to Change Things When Change is Hard.* New York, NY: Broadway Books, 2010.

Kennedy, D. James and Jerry Newcombe. *What If Jesus Had Never Been Born?* Colorado Springs, CO: Thomas Nelson, 1994.

Lamott, Anne. *Bird by Bird: Some Instructions on Writing and Life.* New York, NY: Random House, 1995.

Lewis, C.S. *Mere Christianity.* 1952. New York, NY: HarperCollins, 2001.

Manning, Brennan. *The Ragamuffin Gospel: Good News for the Bedraggled, Beat-Up, and Burnt Out.* Colorado Springs, CO: Multnomah, 2005.

Peterson, Eugene. *Long Obedience in the Same Direction: Discipleship in an Instant Society.* 1980. Downers Grove, IL: InterVarsity Press, 2000.

Piper, John. *The Pleasures of God: Meditations on God's Delight in Being God.* Sisters, OR: Multnomah, 2000.

Robinson, Marilynne. *Gilead: A Novel.* New York, NY: Picador, 2004.

Smedes, Lewis. *A Pretty Good Person: What It Takes to Live with Courage, Gratitude and Integrity.* New York, NY: HarperCollins, 1991.

Stearns, Rich. *The Hole in Our Gospel: What Does God Expect of Us? The Answer That Changed My Life and Might Just Change the World.* Colorado Springs, CO: Thomas Nelson, 2009.

FILMS:

Absolute Power. Dir. Clint Eastwood. With Clint Eastwood, Gene Hackman, and Ed Harris. Castle Rock, 1997.

The Kid. Dir. John Turteltaub. With Bruce Willis and Spencer Breslin. Walt Disney, 2000.

The Shawshank Redemption. Dir. Frank Darabont. With Tim Robbins and Morgan Freeman. Castle Rock, 1994.

Yes Man. Dir. Peyton Reed. With Jim Carrey, Zooey Deschanel, and Bradley Cooper. Warner Bros., 2008.

OTHER MEDIA:

Lewis, Robert. *The Quest for Authentic Manhood Bible Study & DVD Pack.* Lifeway: 2004.

Mahlum, Anne. http://www.backonmyfeet.org/

ABOUT THE AUTHOR

David Peterson was born and raised in Oregon and assumed he would live in that glorious part of the world all of his life. But the wind of the Spirit blew him down other forks in the road to serve as pastor of congregations in Washington, Nevada, Michigan, and finally Texas, where he currently serves as Senior Pastor of the 4,400 member Memorial Drive Presbyterian Church of Houston. He has a B.S. from Lewis and Clark College, an M. Div. from San Francisco Theological Seminary, a D. Min. from Western Theological, and a D.H.L. from Austin College. He has also done post-graduate work at New College, University of Edinburgh, Scotland. He has served on many boards and has extensive involvements in the cities where he has served as well as in renewal efforts within his denomination. David and Terri have been married more than forty years, and they have four children and four grandchildren.